D0754706

KASHMIRI CUISINE

SARLA RAZDAN

KASHMIRI CUISINE
THROUGH THE AGES

Foreword by M.J. Akbar

Lustre Press
Roli Books

Spinning a charkha *in the century gone by.*

DEDICATION

The book is dedicated to Babuji who virtually adopted me as his daughter from the day I joined the Razdan family as his son's bride. He had great taste for food and enjoyed my cooking. It was he who suggested that I should write a book like this. He was the true inspiration and my motivation behind this book. My regret is that I could not do so in his lifetime.

ACKNOWLEDGEMENT

My thanks to Neelesh, Nidhi, Nitin, and Raka for appreciating my work in the kitchen and for helping me with my laptop. And, of course, my husband, M. K. Razdan without his encouragement and help this book would not have been complete. And how can I forget my able lieutenant of years in the kitchen, Ram Saran and Sharvan!

CONTENTS

FOREWORD
M. J. AKBAR

If music, pointed out Shakespeare, was the food of love then clearly the best thing to do was to play on. In the case of the Sarla and M. K. Razdan, food is the music of love, and who can blame M. K. for eating on when he is in married to one of the finest chefs of Kashmiri cuisine!

The quality of food is, without doubt, one of the high points of any civilization. There are of course chefs of genius in any society, but the distinctive feature of the art of cooking is that it is an anonymous art. The chefs of the Nawabs of Awadh, as Abdul Halim Sharar notes, might be able to turn the ordinary dal into an expression of sublime worth, but the more important fact was that anyone with a kitchen in Lucknow made dal and biryani and kofta and kebab of a consistently high quality.

Cooking is a generational art, passed down: Sarla Razdan learnt from her mother, who would, as she says, spend hours making *haak* and *batta* so that her daughter could eat lunch at nine in the morning and then walk the four kilometers to college. This book is, in a sense, a tribute to her mother and to her mother-in-law; but also the distillation of an ageless craft that travels through the past towards an unknown beginning. Who first cooked that supreme *kabargah* or *yakhni*? Who was the original Kashmiri Pandit waaza? The point of course is that it does not matter. Nor does the contemporary waaza at a Kashmir or Kolkata family wedding leave his signature on a meal; cooking is a selfless joy. The true pleasure of the cook lies not in eating what he has made himself, but in offering it to dozens or hundreds or thousands. The great cooks have pride, but no ego.

It is only current capitalism that has given us the phenomenon of chefs who offer 'signature' dishes, but that has more to do with capitalism than with the dish. The false ego on display in Michelin-starred restaurants is only a means of extortion; they do not give to each according to their need [the principle of an Indian dinner, in which the guest is revered], but they certainly take from each customer according to his ability to pay. Those who do not have the ability to pay do not enter the restaurant. [In most countries in the West it is compulsory to mention prices on a menu posted at the door as governments do what they can to curb potential exploitation.]

My own relationship with Kashmiri food, alas, has been intermittent rather than regular. My mother,

Imtiaz, was a Kashmiri, but she was married into a Bihari family living some thirty miles north of Kolkata, so her kofta had to coexist with *chokha*. As a child of mixed ethnic parentage, I can affirm that the combination lifted the joy and savour of both. Fundamentalists will, of course, object, but trust me: try *shalgam gosht* with *baigan bharta* and taste the difference. I have only faint memories of my grandmother, an undiluted Kashmiri whose happy demeanor and comfortable girth indicated a well-fed life. She created a form of cultural angst in my hometown, Telinipara, by drinking pink, salted tea. But the Kashmiri side of the family certainly scored at festive moments like Eid or Bakrid, particularly the latter, when there was plenty of meat left over even after enough had been distributed to ensure that no one in our *mohalla* went without meat that day: food was sent to everyone, Muslims who could not afford to sacrifice a goat, and to non-Muslims who were not vegetarian. The vegetarians got *firni* or *kheer*. Given the fact that all our neighbours were Bihari in this working class jute mill settlement, the truth is that if they received an invitation to eat at our home they expected, and virtually demanded, the exotic flavours of Kashmiri or Punjabi food. After all, they could cook Bihari meals at home.

Demand ensured a steady supply, and my mother, but naturally, passed on her expertise to whoever wanted to learn. There was, as I have mentioned, no ego; and the idea of copyright would have left my mother bemused, if not totally angry.

Time moves on, and culture adopts nuances that might have been inconceivable but a generation before. We can now preserve knowledge in a more distributive way than family inheritance, and a book is among the more noble achievements of humankind. The preservation of Sarla Razdan's genius in between such finely produced covers is a fitting tribute to her, and a blessing to those who would aspire to waft in the odours of her brilliance. One of the great wonders of modern India is the manner in which cuisine has been released from its ethnic and geographical barriers: the *dosa* is in wondrous demand on the road from Delhi to Agra. Kashmiri food, once only on offer in homes, is now a bestseller at catered parties in the capital. People are still a trifle inhibited about cooking it, because, like any delicacy, it demands a delicate sense of the instinct after you have measured ingredients by the spoon or the ladle. But Sarla Razdan's book will chip away the inhibitions and introduce you to a world that cannot be described at the inadequate level of mere words.

The wide, swift-flowing, muddy but picturesque Jhelum River sweeps through ancient Srinagar.

A flower-laden boat in the backwaters of Dal Lake.
Photograph: Steve Mccurry

Author's Note

Lunch at 9 am. That is my earliest food memory from Kashmir.

When I was a little girl in Srinagar, my mother used to spend hours cooking the simplest of things like *haak* (collard greens) and *batta* (rice) for her three children. A pressure cooker was, of course, a dream.

So lunch was at nine in the morning, to arm us for the rest of the day, as we left home. Stuffed with my mother's, simple but delicious food, I then used to walk about 4 km to reach my college. In the winters, I would wake up in the morning to find three to four feet of snow all around. It used to be a lot of fun to play with the snow and we would make snowmen, putting lumps of coal for his eyes. It was freezing – but less so because our mother would wake up much before us and make sure that *kangris* (portable fire pot) were lit up and warming us by the time all of us woke up cribbing and whining.

I am a Kashmiri Pandit. We are called Saraswat Brahmins. Some are vegetarian (to the extent that they don't even have onions or tomatoes), but vast majority are voracious non-vegetarians, like most Kashmiris.

The Shivratri festival called 'Heret' in Kashmir is a big Pandit festival. Some Kashmiri Pandits – also called 'Battas' would eat meat (they were referred to as Nen (meat) Battas and also offer meat to please the gods. The vegetarian Pandits were referred to as Dal (pulses) Battas. Some Kashmiris cooked non-vegetarian food the day after the puja (*Salaam*) as on this day, their Muslim friends would come to greet them and enjoy the festivities.

My maternal home was Dal Battas and my paternal home was Nene Battas. I loved celebrating Shivratri at my maternal home (though I don't know why – as I love my meat cuisine) and I was not allowed to go to my paternal home as they were Nen Battas.

Pandit weddings were a lot of fun. Guests sat on carpets, as they still do in many Kashmiri weddings, and food was served in large *thalis* by waazas (chefs) and family members. It was the same at Muslim weddings, the only difference being the use of the large *trami* (big copper platter) to serve food (one *trami* would be shared by 4 people). That remains largely the tradition even now.

Food was served in several courses. *Kabargah* (fried breast meat) was served with pulao; likewise each dish with its flavour and delicacy was relished and appreciated separately. Liquor and

Atal Bihari Vajpayee

New Delhi
13th March 2008

I had the pleasure of dining with the Razdan family in New York and it was a real treat. The world is full of Indian restaurants but it is not often that one gets to taste authentic cuisine from our country. Mrs. Razdan had prepared an all-Kashmiri meal and there was a lot to choose from. I liked 'haak' saag and, among non-vegetarian dishes 'kabargah', in particular. To get such truly authentic Kashmiri food in the far off US was doubly delightful.

******

Author with the then Prime Minister Shri A B. Vajpayee.

wines were rarely served. *Kehwa* (Kashmiri tea) was and is still served at the weddings.

Pandits celebrate birthdays by cooking *tahar* (yellow rice), which was shared with the family – and in my childhood, the neighbourhood too – after offering it to birds or performing puja. This was one activity which I enjoyed most. Going from one home to another, I distributed yellow rice and met everyone in the process. It was real fun.

During the holy month of Ramzan, the Kashmiri Muslims were woken by a *chowkidar* (watch guard) at four in the morning, as he passed the lanes saying '*Jago!*' As a child, I used to get scared, wondering why the man was shouting at 4 am. I came to know that this was the alarm for our Muslim brethren to have their meal called *sehri*. For the rest of the day, they were not supposed to eat anything, not even water, till 6 pm. A month of fasting was followed by the festival of Eid – everybody from young to old dressed in new clothes, went to mosques, and wished and greeted each other. Pandits and Muslims greeted each other, and children and ladies sang and danced the Rauf. I really miss those days.

Time passed, and I also began cooking the same Kashmiri food I had feasted on as a child. My enthusiasm for cooking really took off when I got married into a family that appreciated and enjoyed good food. My mother-in-law, Somawati, herself cooked some excellent Kashmiri dishes. My husband, M. K. Razdan, in particular, is a connoisseur. He said that I had culinary magic in my hands although he blames me whenever he puts on weight! Praise – and sometimes criticism – from my husband has always guided me towards refining my recipes, and I really thank him for that. He gave a lot of invaluable suggestions that vastly improved the book – especially the one to include low-calorie Kashmiri dishes.

I had the privilege of cooking for guests who were closely known to my husband, especially when they visited us in London and New York where we lived for several years. The little Kashmiri girl in me was mesmerized – these were names I had read only in newspapers, and now they were at our dining table, coming to compliment me in our kitchen!

I remember when Atal Bihari Vajpayee *ji*, former Prime Minister of India, had dinner with us, I had cooked ten dishes – both vegetarian and non-vegetarian. He liked *haak* and *kabargah* and asked me, 'Did you cook all the dishes on your own?'

'Yes,' I said, beaming. He really put his hand on my head and blessed me, saying, 'Bada swadisht khanna' (really delicious food).

When Lata Mangeshkar *ji*, one of the best-known and respected playback singers in India, came to my house I was dying with excitement – my idol was coming over, in flesh and blood! I never dreamt of meeting her when I was growing up in Kashmir and listening to her songs. I have always been a great fan of hers.

And then, like a dream, there she was in the kitchen, saying, 'Can I help in any way?'

Then she asked me: 'Can you make *kehwa* in a *samovar* (brass kettle)?'

I quickly answered, 'Of course!'

The grand promise came easy, but this was Manhattan – where would I get coal in New York to keep the tea hot in the *samovar*, as we did back home. I managed the *kehwa* – without the coal, and she was very happy with it. Her favourite Kashmiri dishes are *rogan josh* and *kabargah* topped with a sweet dish called *shufta*.

And one fine day, I cooked all day without knowing who the guest was. It was Sachin Tendulkar (an Indian cricketer widely regarded as the greatest batsmen in the history of cricket)! His visit – at my New Delhi home – was a huge

Lata Mangeshkar

101, PRABHU KUNJ,
PEDDER ROAD,
MUMBAI - 400 026

FO

Kashmiri food has the reputation of being exotic, hot and essentially non-vegetarian. Some of this reputation is deserved but some is based on misconceptions. Years ago when I was invited to a Kashmiri meal by Sarla Razdan and her husband at their residence in London I asked a few questions about Kashmiri food. The Razdans had questions of their own such as: do I like spicy food? When I said yes, they appeared somewhat surprised because they thought that spicy food may not be good for my vocal cords. They offered to prepare a milder version of Kashmiri food, but I would have none of that. I said I am fond of spicy food and would love to have some 'Rogan Josh'. And did I enjoy the meal! I truly did. Later when I went to New York to perform at the Madison Square Gardens I virtually invited myself to another meal with the Razdan family which, by then, had moved there. This time no questions were asked about my preferences and I was treated to a wonderful meal again. 'Rogan Josh' and 'Kabargah' were very much on the menu. But to the delight of my sister Usha and me there were some very tasty vegetarian dishes which both of us savoured. There was the evergreen and leafy 'Haak', 'Palak and Nadroo' and amazing 'Guchhi'. Having been thus initiated into Kashmiri cuisine, I have never missed an opportunity to enjoy it at any given opportunity.

When I learnt that Sarla is doing a book on Kashmiri cuisine with emphasis on healthy food, I heartily welcomed it. We are all becoming more and more health conscious. While we must enjoy what we eat, we have to keep in mind our health. To some healthy Kashmiri food may appear to be a contradiction in terms. But that is not so as this book proves. I commend it. Read it and enjoy delightful and healthy Kashmiri cuisine.

(Lata Mangeshkar)
28·08·08

Author with the melody queen Lata Mangeshkar at her home.

> " I discovered the great taste of Kashmiri food at a dinner with the Razdan family. 'Kabargah', made out of lamb's breast boiled in milk before frying, was truely mouth-watering. So was 'Yakhni', lamb cooked in yoghurt. I could not resist requesting Mrs Razdan for recipes of at least 4 of the dishes she had cooked. I tried my hand at these dishes at my home in Mumbai. I did not do a bad job but was no match to the culinary skills of Mrs Razdan!"

Sachin Tendulkar

Author with Sachin Tendulkar.

surprise. I was not told who the guest was because I might have blabbed away to my friends, and a crowd would have collected if word spread.

After dinner, he requested me for four recipes, including *yakhni* and *kabargah*. I gave him the same recipes that I had written for this book; he tried making them at home and gave me his feedback as well. I hope my readers enjoy making them like Sachin did, hopefully with better results!

Kashimiris are hospitable by nature. We enjoy socialising and entertaining. I am no different. Frankly speaking, if one enjoys good food, then one enjoys cooking too. Cooking is my hobby, it is a great source of pleasure to cook for my family and friends.

Kashmir is unique in many ways – its natural beauty and the way Hindus and Muslims live together, notwithstanding the turbulent times the State has witnessed in recent years. We Pandits grew up in Muslim neighbourhoods. We shared the same language, the same music, and went to the same schools. Pandit and Muslim cuisines, however, are different – each special in its own way. The Muslim cuisine is overwhelmingly non-vegetarian, whereas the Pandits enjoy non-vegetarian dishes and also a wide variety of vegetarian food. A Muslim wedding in the neighbourhood provided a strong challenge to the taste buds – the Wazwaan, with over 30 varieties of meat preparation is truly a gastronomic Olympiad. Our Muslim neighbours would always invite us to savour this delightful food. For those who could not make it, food would be sent home.

When I grew up, I never stopped asking questions from my Muslim friends about how they would go about preparing such delicacies. I have included some of those recipes herein. I hope I have been able to do some justice to the reputation of Wazwaan.

I have also tried to devise innovative methods

of making Kashmiri cooking simple and more adaptable without compromising on its taste.

Today, people like to eat good food, but don't have enough time to cook. I want to help our younger generation stay in touch with their finger-licking tradition of food. This book will help the younger generation (time-conscious old generation as well) to cook Kashmiri food, host parties, without investing too much time, yet keeping up with the taste.

I have also tried to introduce some dishes for the calorie-conscious readers. After all, there are a lot of myths attached to Kashmiri cuisine: that it is time consuming to make and oily to eat – tasty yet unhealthy. With this book, I have tried to iron out all these misconceptions. I have offered what I felt is an easier approach to Kashmiri cooking – a little less spice here, a little less oil there, using modern ways of cooking, and making the same centuries-old Kashmiri cooking modern and trendier.

Bon apetit!

डा. फारुक अब्दुल्ला
Dr. FAROOQ ABDULLAH

मंत्री
नवीन और नवीकरणीय ऊर्जा
भारत सरकार
MINISTER
NEW AND RENEWABLE ENERGY
GOVERNMENT OF INDIA

January 17, 2010

Kashmir is famous for its beauty, arts and craft although unfortunately it has been in the news for the wrong reason in recent years. Kashmir food is a work of art by itself. Who does not love a 'Gushtaba' and a whole lot of other delicacies! I should know because I have been a willing 'victim' of these mouth-watering dishes. If I have any reservations about Kashmiri food it is that the best dishes are mutton based, something doctors advise not to over indulge in. Although a trained doctor myself I selectively listen to the Doctor! Such is the temptation of Kashmiri food!

I am, therefore doubly delighted that the book that Sarla Razdan has authored maintains a balance between what the doctors advise and what taste buds salivate for! Her stress on healthy Kashmiri food is welcome at a time when everyone is becoming more and more health conscious. That makes the book unique. I do intend to try out many of these recipes.

(Farooq Abdullah)

BASIC PREPARATIONS

GARAM MASALA
Makes: 500 gm / 1.1 lb

Take 250 gm / 9 oz cumin (*jeera*) seeds, 10 cloves (*laung*), 3 tbsp nutmeg (*jaiphal*) powder, 5 tbsp cinnamon (*dalchini*), 5 tbsp black cardamom (*badi elaichi*) seeds, 5 tbsp green cardamom (*choti elaichi*) seeds, 4 bay leaves (*tej patta*), 3 tbsp black cumin (*shah jeera*) seeds, 250 gm / 9 oz fenugreek seeds (*methi dana*), and 250 gm / 9 oz coriander (*dhaniya*) seeds.

Powder all these spices in a grinder and sift through a mesh cloth. Store in an airtight jar. Use as required.

VER MASALA
(Spice cake)

There are two types of *ver masala* – the one made with asafoetida is generally used in Pandit cuisine, while the other one is made with garlic and shallots and is popular in Wazwaan cooking.

Ver Masala with Asafoetida

Take ½ cup / 110 ml / 3½ fl oz mustard oil, ½ cup asafoetida (*hing*) liquid, 2 tsp salt, ½ cup red chilli powder, ½ cup / 100 gm / 3½ oz black gram (*urad dal*), ground, 2 tsp / 6 gm crushed black cumin (*shah jeera*) seeds, 2 tbsp black cardamom (*badi elaichi*) powder, 2 tbsp cinnamon (*dalchini*) powder, 2 tbsp clove (*laung*) powder, 3 tbsp cumin (*jeera*) seeds, 2 tbsp nutmeg (*jaiphal*) powder, 5 tsp /

15 gm fennel (*saunf*) powder, 50 gm / 1¾ oz ginger powder (*sonth*), 2 cups / 500 ml / 16 fl oz water, 30 gm / 1 oz coriander (*dhaniya*) powder, and 3 tsp garam masala powder.

Mix all the ingredients in a large pot. Rub in mustard oil till well incorporated. Add asafoetida liquid, gradually, rubbing and mixing really well and make a hard dough. Divide the dough equally into portions and shape each into a 3″-thick, round cake. Spread the cakes on a greased plate and sun-dry for a day, turning them once. Dry till the moisture evaporates and the cakes become stiff. Store in an airtight jar and refrigerate.

Ver Masala with Garlic and Shallots
Makes: 1 kg / 2.2 lb

Take 100 gm / 3½ oz ground garlic (*lasan*), 100 gm / 3½ oz peeled and ground shallots, 25 gm salt, 10 gm crushed black cumin (*shah jeera*) seeds, 250 gm / 9 oz ground black gram, 50 gm / 1¾ oz crushed cumin (*jeera*) seeds, 100 gm / 3½ oz ginger powder (*sonth*), 100 gm / 3½ oz fennel (*saunf*) powder, 250 gm / 9 oz coriander (*dhaniya*) seeds, 50 gm / 1¾ oz turmeric (*haldi*) powder, 150 gm / 5 oz red chilli powder, 100 gm / 3½ oz ground cloves (*laung*), ½ cup

/ 110 ml/ 3½ fl oz mustard oil, and 1 cup / 250 ml/ 8 fl oz water.

Mix all the ingredients in a deep pot along with water and knead to make a stiff dough. Divide the dough equally into small portions and shape into cakes. Dry the cakes in the sun until they have no moisture left. Store in an air-tight jar. Break about 10 gm of cake and coarsely crush between the palms and add to the desired dish in the last step.

ASAFOETIDA LIQUID

Soak the asafoetida stone in warm water in a container and refrigerate. Use whenever needed.

HOME MADE YOGHURT

Take 1 lt/ 32 fl oz milk & 3 tbsp/ 45 gm/ 1½ oz yoghurt (*dahi*).

Boil the milk, remove from heat and let it cool to room temperature. Pour in a glass jar or in a jar made of baked clay. Even pearl pet containers will do. Mix yoghurt with the milk and cover with a lid. Wrap in a shawl or old blanket for 4 hours or overnight. In summers you do not need any wrapping.

TIPS FOR CLEANING LOTUS STEMS, HAAK AND OTHER LEAFY VEGETABLES

1 Scrape lotus stems and cut into the shape desired (lotus stem is cut in different shapes for different dishes). Clean under running tap water so that all the mud comes out.
2 *Haak* is a leafy vegetable of Kashmir. Sort out leaves preferably curly ones and cut the stems out. Wash in a large pot till it is clean. You can use a pinch of potassium permaganate. Soak *haak* in potassium permaganate for 5 minutes and wash in lot of water till clean. If you cannot find *haak* you can use spinach instead.

TIPS ON HOW TO USE AND PRESERVE MUSTARD OIL

1 Heat 2 lt or 5 lt mustard oil in a large wok (*kadhai*) till smoking.
2 To check if the oil is ready to use or the smoke has gone completely put ½ peeled potato in it, if it turns brown the oil is done.
3 Let the oil cool down completely and store in a jar. Use as required. You can save lot of time by heating and storing it in advance.

17

SNACKS

Tailors and embroiderers at work under the shade of the Chinar tree in the early twentieth century.

Seekh Kabab

SKEWERED MINCED LAMB

Serves: 6

INGREDIENTS

1 kg / 2.2 lb Minced
   meat from leg of lamb
   done 5 times
3 tsp / 9 gm Red chilli powder
4 tsp Amul cheese, grated
1 tsp / 6 gm Garlic (*lasan*) paste
1 tsp / 6 gm Ginger (*adrak*) paste
3 Green chillies, cut into small pieces
1 tsp / 3 gm Black cardamom (*badi elaichi*)
   powder
Salt to taste
3½ tbsp / 50 gm / 1¾ oz Butter
2 Eggs, beaten
1 tsp / 3 gm Dry mint (*pudina*)
2 tsp / 6 gm Cumin (*jeera*) powder
2 tbsp / 8 gm Green coriander (*hara dhaniya*),
   chopped

METHOD

1 In a bowl, mix the mince, red chilli powder, cheese, garlic paste, ginger paste, green chillies, black cardamom powder, salt, butter, eggs, mint, cumin powder, and green coriander with your hands.

2 Take medium-sized skewers, 1˝ in diameter, and cover the middle portion with a handful of minced meat pressing with moist hands so that it sticks.

3 Place the skewers on charcoal fire or in a pre heated oven at 230°C / 450°F. Keep checking till they are grilled all around.

4 When the kebabs are brown, slide them slowly into a serving dish. Repeat with the remaining mince.

5 Serve as a snack or with the main course.

Kanti

BONELESS LAMB CUBES

Serves: 6

INGREDIENTS

1 kg / 2.2 lb Lamb, boneless,
   cut into 2 cm cubes, washed
3 tbsp / 45 ml / 1½ fl oz Mustard oil
500 gm / 1.1 lb Onions, peeled, cut into 4 pieces
1 cup Tomatoes, chopped
1 tsp / 3 gm Red chilli powder
1 tsp / 3 gm Ginger powder (*sonth*)
Salt to taste
1 tsp / 5 ml Lemon (*nimbu*) juice

METHOD

1 Heat the oil in a pressure cooker; add meat cubes and semi-fry till the water dries up. Add onions and tomatoes; stir well. Add red chilli powder, ginger powder, and salt; pressure cook for 5 minutes. Remove the lid of the cooker. Add lemon juice and simmer for 5 minutes.

2 Serve as a cocktail snack or at tea time.

Gaad Talith t, Badam

FRIED FISH WITH ALMONDS

Serves: 6

INGREDIENTS

1 kg / 2.2 lb Fish, boneless, cut into triangular
  or square pieces
Salt to taste
1 tsp / 3 gm Black pepper (*kali mirch*)
6 tbsp / 100 gm / 3½ oz Butter
½ cup / 60 gm / 2 oz All purpose flour (*maida*)
½ cup / 70 gm / 2¼ oz Almond (*badam*) flakes

METHOD

1 Wash the fish and sprinkle salt and black pepper.
   Keep aside for 1 hour.

2 Heat the butter in a frying pan; coat the fish
   with the flour and fry each side for 3 minutes on
   medium heat. While frying, add some almond
   flakes.

3 Remove and decorate with slices of lemon and
   lettuce leaves.

4 Serve hot as a snack or with the main course.

Al Posh Mond

FRIED PUMPKIN FLOWER

Serves: 6

INGREDIENTS

250 gm / 9 oz Pumpkin flower, washed,
  drained
Salt to taste
½ tsp / 1½ gm Red chilli powder
½ cup / 60 gm / 2 oz Rice flour
2 cups / 440 ml / 15 fl oz Refined oil for frying

METHOD

1 Take 1 cup water in a bowl, add salt, red chilli
   powder, and rice flour. Mix well to make a not
   so thick paste.

2 Mix the pumpkin flower with the paste.

3 Heat the oil in a pan; fry the flowers till crispy
   brown. Remove and drain the excess oil on
   absorbent kitchen towels.

4 Serve as a snack with tea or cocktails or
   main course.

Wangen Pakora

FRIED AUBERGINE COATED WITH GRAM FLOUR

Serves: 6

INGREDIENTS

1 kg / 2.2 lb Aubergine (*baigan*), washed, cut
  into round thin slices
1 cup / 150 gm / 5 oz Gram flour (*besan*)
1 tsp / 3 gm Red chilli powder
Salt to taste
2 cups / 440 ml / 15 fl oz Refined oil for frying

METHOD

1 In a bowl, mix gram flour, red chilli powder,
   salt, and aubergine together. Add 1 cup water
   and mix well to make a batter of normal
   consistency.

2 Heat the oil in a pan; fry the aubergine till crisp
   and brown. Remove and drain the excess oil on
   absorbent kitchen towels.

3 Serve hot as a snack or as an accompaniment with
   the main course.

Nadir Churma

LOTUS STEM CHIPS

Serves: 6

INGREDIENTS

1 kg / 2.2 lb Lotus stems (*kamal kakri*), cut into
  2-3 cm-long pieces, washed, drained
3 cups / 660 ml / 21 fl oz Refined oil for frying
Salt to taste
¼ tsp Red chilli powder

METHOD

1 In a pot, put lotus stem and water to cover; boil
   for 10 minutes. Drain well in a colander and
   keep aside to cool.

2 Heat the oil in a deep pan; fry the lotus chips
   till crispy golden brown. Remove and drain on
   absorbent tissue paper.

3 Sprinkle salt and red chilli powder; mix well
   and serve hot as a snack or with main course.

Nadir Monjvor

LOTUS STEM CUTLETS

Serves: 6

INGREDIENTS

500 gm / 1.1 lb Lotus stems (*kamal kakri*),
  scraped, washed, grated
1 tsp / 3 gm Ginger powder (*sonth*)
2 tsp / 6 gm Red chilli powder
Salt to taste
2 tbsp / 20 gm Rice flour / Corn flour
1 cup / 220 ml / 7 fl oz Refined oil for frying

METHOD

1 Squeeze the water out of the grated lotus stems.

2 In a bowl, mix the grated lotus stem, ginger
   powder, red chilli powder, salt, and rice flour
   together.

3 Divide the mixture into equal portions and
   shape into small balls and flatten slightly.

4 Heat the oil in a frying pan; fry these cutlets till
   crispy brown, turning once or twice. Repeat
   with the remaining balls.

5 Serve hot as a snack or with the main course.

Top: Gujjar women.
Below: Kashmiri papier maché merchant from 1890's.

23

A picturesque autumn scene in Srinagar when the green leaves turn to gold and then to russet and red.
Photograph: Mukhtar Ahmad

*Silver and coppersmiths chasing, gliding and polishing
decorative articles like tea sets, tumblers, boxes, and more in
the early days.*

Lamb

28 **MACH SHYAMI**
Minced lamb cutlets in yoghurt

29 **MACHGAND**
Minced lamb fingers

30 **MACH T, CHER**
Lamb fingers with apricot

31 **OLUV BUKHARA BARITH MACH**
Apricot stuffed meat balls

32 **METHI T GOLEMACH**
Lamb balls in fenugreek sauce

32 **MACH T, MACARONI**
Minced lamb in macaroni

33 **MACH BARITH KAREL**
Bitter gourd stuffed with minced lamb

33 **MACH T, PHOOL**
Lamb fingers with cauliflower

35 **MACH T, OLUV**
Lamb fingers cooked with potatoes

36 **METHI T, SYUN**
Fenugreek cooked with lamb

36 **MUNJ T, SYUN**
Knol khol cooked with lamb

37 **YAKHNI**
Lamb cooked in yoghurt

38 **GUSHTABA**
Lamb balls in yoghurt gravy

39 **RISTA**
Lamb balls in red gravy

42 **PALAK T, RISTA**
Lamb balls cooked with spinach

43 **KABARGAH**
Lamb chunks decorated with silver leaf

43 **AAB GOSHT**
Lamb in milk gravy

46 **DHANIWAL KORMA**
Lamb in coriander flavoured gravy

46 **ALUBUKHAR KORMA**
Lamb cooked with plums

47 **PALAK T, SYUN**
Spinach cooked with lamb

47 **GOLE AL SYUN**
Pumpkin cooked with lamb

48 **KALIYA**
Lamb in yellow gravy

48 **ROGAN JOSH**
Lamb in red gravy

49 **GOGJI T, SYUN**
Lamb with turnips

49 **VOST HAAK T, SYUN**
Green /red leaves with lamb

52 **OLUV T, SYUN**
Potatoes and lamb in thick gravy

52 **CHAMP**
Lamb chops

53 **BUKVETCH CHAGIL T, CHARVAN**
Spicy kidneys, testes and liver

53 **TCHOKH CHARVAN**
Tangy liver

55 **PACHH ROGAN JOSH**
Trotter in red gravy

55 **PACHH RAS**
Trotter soup

Mach Shyami

MINCED LAMB CUTLETS IN YOGHURT

Serves: 6-10

INGREDIENTS

1 kg / 2.2 lb Minced lamb
3 tsp / 9 gm Fennel (*saunf*) powder
2 tsp / 6 gm Ginger powder (*sonth*)
½ cup / 110 ml / 3½ fl oz Mustard / Refined oil
Salt to taste
½ tsp Asafoetida (*hing*)
3 Cloves (*laung*)
2 Bay leaves (*tej patta*)
2 pieces Cinnamon (*dalchini*) sticks
2 tsp / 6 gm Cumin (*jeera*) powder
3 cups / 675 gm / 24 oz Yoghurt (*dahi*),
   whisked
3 Black cardamoms (*badi elaichi*)
4 Green cardamoms (*choti elaichi*)
2 tsp / 5 gm Black cumin (*shah jeera*) seeds

METHOD

1 In a large bowl, mix the minced meat with 1 tsp fennel power, ½ tsp ginger powder, and ½ tsp salt. Divide the mixture into two to three portions and shape into 4˝-long rolls.

2 Boil 8 cups water separately in a large vessel, put the rolls in the water carefully so that they don't break. Boil till the rolls are hard; remove the vessel from the heat and keep aside to cool.

3 Take the rolls out of the vessel and preserve the stock. Cut these rolls into 1½ ˝ round cutlets.

4 Heat the oil in a deep vessel; add salt, asafoetida, cloves, bay leaves, and cinnamon sticks. Add the preserved stock and the remaining fennel powder, ginger powder and cumin powder; bring the mixture to the boil.

5 Add the whisked yoghurt to the gravy and let it boil till the gravy thickens.

6 Add the minced meat cutlets to the mixture and bring to the boil.

7 Grind black cardamoms and green cardamoms together, along with the skin. Add to the gravy along with black cumin seeds; mix well.

8 Serve hot with steamed rice, chapatti or *nan*.

Note: This dish is served on very special occasions like weddings and festivals.

Machgand
MINCED LAMB FINGERS

Serves: 6-10

INGREDIENTS

1 kg / 2.2 lb Minced meat from leg of lamb
3 tsp / 9 gm Red chilli powder
2 tsp / 6 gm Ginger powder (*sonth*)
3 tsp / 9 gm Fennel (*saunf*) powder
Salt to taste
4 Black cardamoms (*badi elaichi*)
3 tsp / 9 gm White cumin seed powder
1 cup / 220 ml / 7 fl oz Mustard oil
¼ tsp Asafoetida (*hing*) liquid (see p. 17)
2 Bay leaves (*tej patta*)
2 Cloves (*laung*)
3 Green cardamoms (*choti elaichi*)

A flower seller on the Dal Lake at winter time.

METHOD

1 Mix the minced meat with 1 tsp red chilli powder, ½ tsp ginger powder, 1 tsp fennel powder, 1 tsp salt, 3 ground black cardamom, 1 tsp cumin powder, and 3 tbsp mustard oil in a large bowl. Marinate for 10 minutes.

2 Divide the mixture equally into 25 portions and shape into 1½″-long fingers.

3 Heat the remaining mustard oil in a deep vessel. Add salt, asafoetida liquid, bay leaves, cloves, 1 cup water, and remaining red chilli powder.

4 Keep stirring on high heat till the water is absorbed and the mixture turns red. Pour 6 cups water and add remaining spice powders and salt to taste; bring to the boil.

5 Add minced meat fingers, one by one, into the gravy. Let it boil on high heat till it leaves oil.

6 Coarsely grind green cardamom and 1 black cardamom together and add to the vessel; mix. Serve hot.

Note: Chilli and salt can be altered to taste without spoiling the delicate flavour of this dish. If you are unable to shape the mince into fingers, round balls can be made instead.

Mach t, Cher

LAMB FINGERS WITH APRICOT

Serves: 6-10

INGREDIENTS

1 kg / 2.2 lb Minced lamb
500 gm / 1.1 lb Yellow dried apricot (*khubani*),
    washed in lukewarm water
1 cup / 220 ml / 7 fl oz Mustard / Refined oil
2 tsp / 6 gm Ginger powder (*sonth*)
3 tsp / 9 gm Red chilli powder
3 tsp / 9 gm Fennel (*saunf*) powder
Salt to taste
2 tsp / 6 gm White cumin seed powder
3 Black cardamoms (*badi elaichi*)
½ tsp Asafoetida (*hing*) liquid (see p. 17)
2 Cinnamon (*dalchini*) sticks
1 Bay leaf (*tej patta*)
2 Cloves (*laung*)

METHOD

1 Mix the minced meat with 3 tbsp oil, ½ tsp ginger powder, 1 tsp red chilli powder, 1 tsp fennel powder, 1 tsp salt, and 1 tsp cumin powder in a large bowl.

2 Coarsely grind 2 black cardamoms and add to the mixture. Mix well and keep aside to marinate for 10 minutes.

3 Divide the mixture equally into portions and shape into 1½"-long fingers.

4 Heat the remaining oil in a large vessel; add salt, asafoetida liquid, cinnamon sticks, bay leaf, remaining red chilli powder, and ½ cup water. Stir till a red colour appears.

5 Add 6 cups water and the remaining spice powders.

6 When the gravy starts boiling, add the meat fingers slowly so that they don't break. Boil on high heat till the gravy thickens.

7 Add apricots and boil for 2 more minutes. Reduce heat and simmer for 5 minutes and serve.

Note: This dish looks beautiful when laid on the table as the apricots remain yellow and the minced meat red making it very colourful.

Oluv Bukhara Barith Mach

MINCED MEAT BALLS STUFFED WITH APRICOT

Serves: 6-10

INGREDIENTS

1 kg / 2.2 lb Minced lamb

500 gm / 1.1 lb Dried apricots (*khubani*), round ones, soaked for 30 minutes in warm water, deseeded

1 cup / 220 ml / 7 fl oz Mustard / Refined oil

2 tsp / 6 gm Ginger powder (*sonth*)

3 tsp / 9 gm Red chilli powder

3 tsp / 9 gm Fennel (*saunf*) powder

Salt to taste

2 tsp / 6 gm White cumin seed powder

3 tsp / 9 gm Black cardamom (*badi elaichi*) powder

½ tsp Asafoetida (*hing*) liquid (see p. 17)

2 Bay leaves (*tej patta*)

2 Cinnamon (*dalchini*) sticks

METHOD

1 Mix the minced meat with 3 tbsp oil, ½ tsp ginger powder, 1 tsp red chilli powder, 1 tsp fennel powder, 1 tsp salt, 1 tsp cumin powder, and 1½ tsp black cardamom powder. Marinate for 20 minutes

2 Divide the mixture equally into portions and shape into round balls, stuffing an apricot into each ball.

3 Heat the remaining oil in a vessel; add salt, asafoetida liquid, a little water, and 2 tsp red chill powder; bring to the boil till the mixture turns red.

4 Add 6 cups water and remaining spice powders. When the gravy is boiling, add the meat balls gradually so that they don't break. Boil till the gravy thickens. Add remaining cardamom powder and simmer for 5 minutes. Serve hot.

A shikara ride at sunset on the Dal Lake is an unforgettable experience.
Photograph: Mukhtar Ahmad

Methi t, Golemach

MINCED MEAT BALLS WITH FENUGREEK

Serves: 6-8

INGREDIENTS

1 kg / 2.2 lb Minced lamb
6 tsp Dried fenugreek (*kasoori methi*)
Salt to taste
1 tsp / 3 gm Ginger powder (*sonth*)
3 tsp / 9 gm Fennel (*saunf*) powder
3 tsp / 9 gm Red chilli powder
2 Black cardamoms (*badi elaichi*)
3 Green cardamoms (*choti elaichi*)
2 tsp / 6 gm White cumin seed powder
1 cup / 220 ml / 7 fl oz Mustard / Refined oil
1 Bay leaf (*tej patta*)
½ tsp Asafoetida (*hing*)
3 Cloves (*laung*)
2 Cinnamon (*dalchini*) sticks

METHOD

1 Mix the minced meat with 1 tsp salt, ½ tsp ginger powder, 1 tsp fennel powder, 1 tsp red chilli powder, 1 crushed black cardamom, 2 crushed green cardamoms, 1 tsp cumin powder, and 2 tbsp oil in a large bowl. Mix well and marinate for 10 minutes.

2 Divide the mixture equally into portions and shape into 1″-thick balls.

3 Heat the remaining oil in a pot; add bay leaf, asafoetida, cloves, cinnamon sticks, salt to taste, 1 cup water, and 2 tsp red chilli powder. Keep stirring till the mixture turns red.

4 Add 6 cups water and remaining spice powders except the fenugreek powder. Bring the mixture to the boil. Add the meat balls gradually so that they don't break.

5 Boil till the gravy thickens. Add the fenugreek powder and simmer for 5 minutes. Serve hot.

Mach t, Macaroni

MINCED LAMB IN MACARONI

Serves: 6-10

INGREDIENTS

1 kg / 2.2 lb Minced lamb
1 cup / 100 gm / 3½ oz Macaroni, cut, soaked in warm water for 5 minutes, drained in a colander
½ cup / 110 ml / 3½ fl oz Refined oil
1 Clove (*laung*)
1 Cinnamon (*dalchini*) stick
2 cups Tomatoes, fresh, chopped OR
400 gm / 14 oz Tomato purée
Salt to taste
3 tsp / 9 gm Red chilli powder
1 tsp / 3 gm Ginger powder (*sonth*)
3 tsp / 9 gm Cumin (*jeera*) powder
2 tsp / 6 gm Black cardamom (*badi elaichi*) powder

METHOD

1 Heat the oil in a deep vessel; add clove, cinnamon stick, and mince. Fry till the water dries up. Add chopped tomatoes or tomato purée. Keep stirring. Add salt, red chilli powder, ginger powder, cumin powder, and black cardamom powder; mix well. Add 6 cups water and bring the mixture to the boil.

2 Add macaroni and mix well. Bring to boil again for 10 minutes. Simmer for 5 minutes and serve with *nan*, chapatti or rice.

Note: Make sure you buy long-cut macaroni. To prevent the macaroni from getting too soggy keep checking from time to time.

Mach Barith Karel

BITTER GOURD STUFFED WITH MINCED LAMB

Serves: 6

INGREDIENTS

500 gm / 1.1 lb Minced lamb
12 Bitter gourd (*karela*), scraped, slit lengthwise keeping shape intact, deseeded
½ cup / 110 ml / 3½ fl oz Mustard / Refined oil for frying
¼ tsp Asafoetida (*hing*)
Salt to taste
2 tsp / 6 gm Red chilli powder
2 tsp / 6 gm Ginger powder (*sonth*)
2 tsp / 6 gm Cumin (*jeera*) powder

METHOD

1 Sprinkle salt on the bitter gourd and keep aside for an hour. Wash it under running water and squeeze well.

2 Heat the oil in a pan; shallow-fry the bitter gourd till golden brown. Remove and cool.

3 Heat 2 tbsp oil in a pan; add asafoetida, salt to taste, and minced meat. Fry till the mince turns light brown. Add all the powdered spices and ½ cup water; mix well with a ladle and cook till the water dries up. Remove.

4 Stuff the fried bitter gourd with the mince and serve with chapatti, *nan* or rice.

Mach t, Phool

MINCED LAMB FINGERS WITH CAULIFLOWER

Serves: 6-8

INGREDIENTS

1 kg 2.2 lb Minced lamb
500 gm / 1.1 lb Cauliflower (*phool gobi*), cut into medium-sized florets, washed, drained
3 tsp / 9 gm Red chilli powder
3 tsp / 9 gm Fennel (*saunf*) powder
2 tsp / 6 gm Ginger powder (*sonth*)
Salt to taste
2 tsp / 6 gm Cumin (*jeera*) powder
1 cup / 220 ml / 7 fl oz Mustard / Refined oil
¼ tsp Asafoetida (*hing*)
2 Cloves (*laung*)

METHOD

1 Mix the mince with 1 tsp red chilli powder, 1 tsp fennel powder, 1 tsp ginger powder, 1 tsp salt, 1 tsp cumin powder, 3 tbsp oil in a large bowl and keep aside for 30 minutes.

2 Divide the mixture and shape into 1½″-thick fingers.

3 Heat the oil in a large vessel; add salt, asafoetida, cloves, 2 cups water, and remaining red chilli powder. Keep stirring till the mixture turns red. Add 6 cups water and remaining spice powders. Bring to the boil.

4 Add the minced fingers, one by one so that they don't break. Cook for 15 minutes on high heat.

5 Fry the cauliflower light brown in a separate pan and add to the mixture. Cook for 5 minutes and serve with rice, *nan* or chapatti.

Mach t, Oluv

LAMB FINGERS COOKED WITH POTATOES

Serves: 6-8

INGREDIENTS

1 kg / 2.2 lb Minced lamb
500 gm / 1.1 lb Potatoes, peeled, cut into 4
  pieces lengthwise, washed
3 tsp / 9 gm Red chilli powder
3 tsp / 9 gm Fennel (*saunf*) powder
2 tsp / 6 gm Ginger powder (*sonth*)
1 cup / 220 ml / 7 fl oz Mustard / Refined oil
2 Black cardamoms (*badi elaichi*), half ground
2 Bay leaves (*tej patta*)
3 Cloves (*laung*)
2 Cinnamon (*dalchini*) sticks
½ tsp Asafoetida (*hing*)
Salt to taste
1 tsp / 3 gm Black cardamom powder

METHOD

1 Mix the minced lamb with 1 tsp red chilli
  powder, 1 tsp fennel powder, ½ tsp ginger
  powder, 3 tbsp oil, ½ tsp salt, and half ground
  black cardamoms in a large bowl. Mix well
  with hands.

2 Divide the mixture equally into portions and
  make 2½″-long fingers. Keep aside.

3 Fry the potatoes in oil till golden brown. Keep
  aside.

4 In the same oil add bay leaves, cloves, cinnamon
  sticks, asafoetida, salt, ½ cup water, and
  remaining red chilli powder. Bring to the boil
  stirring with a ladle for 2 minutes or till the
  mixture turns red. Add 6 cups water and the
  remaining spice powders and bring to the boil.

5 Add the lamb fingers and boil for 5-7 minutes.
  Remove lid and add the fried potatoes and
  black cardamom powder. Boil for 5 minutes.

6 Serve hot with steamed rice, *nan* or chapatti.

Facing page: Kashmiri children dressed for a photo shoot many decades back.

Methi t, Syun

FENUGREEK COOKED WITH LAMB

Serves: 6

INGREDIENTS

1 kg / 2.2 lb Lamb,
  boneless, cut into
  cubes, washed
1 kg / 2.2 lb Fenugreek
  (*methi*), cleaned, washed,
  drained
1 cup / 220 ml / 7 fl oz Mustard oil
½ tsp Asafoetida (*hing*) liquid (see p. 17)
2 Cloves (*laung*)
2 Cinnamon (*dalchini*) sticks
2 Bay leaves (*tej patta*)
3 tsp / 9 gm Red chilli powder
1 tsp / 3 gm Turmeric (*haldi*) powder
Salt to taste
2 tsp / 6 gm Ginger powder (*sonth*)
3 tsp / 9 gm Fennel (*saunf*) powder
2 tsp / 6 gm Black cardamom (*badi elaichi*)
  powder
2 tsp / 6 gm Cumin (*jeera*) powder

METHOD

1 Boil the fenugreek in a vessel till tender.

2 Heat the oil in a pressure cooker; add asafoetida
  liquid, cloves, cinnamon stick, bay leaves, and
  meat. Fry the meat till golden brown.

3 Add red chilli powder, turmeric powder,
  2 cups water, and salt to taste; stir with a ladle
  on high heat. Add fenugreek and remaining
  spice powders; mix well. Pressure cook for 10
  minutes or till 2 whistles.

4 Remove the lid and check if the meat is tender,
  cook till the gravy thickens.

5 Serve hot with rice, chapatti or *nan*.

Munj t, Syun

KNOL KHOL COOKED WITH LAMB

Serves: 6

INGREDIENTS

1 kg / 2.2 lb Lamb cut from breast and shoulder,
  washed
500 gm / 1.1 lb Knol khol (*kholrabi*), peeled, cut
  into 4 pieces, leaves washed, drained
½ cup / 110 ml / 3½ fl oz Mustard / Refined oil
Salt to taste
½ tsp Asafoetida (*hing*) liquid (see p. 17)
3 tsp / 9 gm Fennel (*saunf*) powder
1½ tsp / 4½ gm Ginger powder (*sonth*)
1½ tsp / 4½ gm Turmeric (*haldi*) powder

METHOD

1 Heat the oil in a pressure cooker; add salt,
  asafoetida, and lamb. Fry for 10 minutes. Add
  knol khol along with the leaves; cook for
  another few seconds.

2 Pour 6 cups water and add the spice powders.
  Pressure cook for 10 minutes and remove the
  lid.

3 Serve with steamed rice.

Yakhni

LAMB COOKED IN YOGHURT

Serves: 6

INGREDIENTS

1 kg / 2.2 lb Lamb cut from breast and shoulder
  with bones, cleaned
½ cup / 110 ml / 3½ fl oz Mustard / Refined oil
1 Cinnamon (*dalchini*) stick
3 Black cardamoms (*badi elaichi*)
4 Green cardamoms (*choti elaichi*)
2 Bay leaves (*tej patta*)
2 Cloves (*laung*)
3 tsp / 9 gm Fennel (*saunf*) powder
2 tsp / 6 gm Ginger powder (*sonth*)
Salt to taste
3 cups / 675 gm / 24 oz Yoghurt (*dahi*)
1 tsp / 5 gm Corn flour / Rice flour
1 tsp / 2½ gm Black cumin (*shah jeera*) seeds

METHODS

1 Heat the oil in a pressure cooker; add cinnamon
   stick, 1 black cardamom, 2 green cardamoms,
   bay leaves, cloves, and lamb. Fry for 10
   minutes.

2 Pour 6 cups water and add fennel powder,
   ginger powder, and salt to taste. Pressure cook
   for 10 minutes or till 2 whistles. Remove the
   lid when the pressure drops and check if the
   meat is tender. Pour the stock out from the
   pressure cooker into a separate vessel and keep
   the meat pieces inside.

3 Whisk the yoghurt in a bowl. Add to the stock,
   stirring with a ladle, and cook till it starts
   boiling. Add the cooked meat and cook till the
   gravy thickens.

4 Whisk 1 tsp corn flour or rice flour in 4 tsp
   water. Add to the meat mixture (this helps in
   thickening the gravy).

5 Coarsely grind 2 black and 2 green cardamoms,
   and add to the gravy. Sprinkle black cumin
   seeds (this gives a wonderful flavour). Serve hot
   with steamed rice.

Note: This is Sachin Tendulkar's favourite dish.

Gushtaba

LAMB BALLS IN YOGHURT GRAVY

Serves: 6-8

INGREDIENTS

1 kg / 2.2 lb Lamb, boneless from leg
250 gm / 9 oz Meat fat / White butter
3 Black cardamoms (*badi elaichi*)
1 tsp / 3 gm Ginger powder (*sonth*)
Salt to taste
10 bones Lamb stock
12 cups / 3 lt Water
½ cup / 100 gm / 3½ oz Ghee
1 tsp / 6 gm Garlic (*lasan*) paste
2 tsp / 6 gm Fried onion paste
2 Cloves (*laung*)
1 Cinnamon (*dalchini*) stick
5 Green cardamoms (*choti elaichi*)
2 Bay leaves (*tej patta*)
3 tsp / 9 gm Fennel (*saunf*) powder
2 cups / 480 ml / 16 fl oz Milk
2 cups / 450 gm / 1 lb Yoghurt (*dahi*)
2 tsp / 6 gm Dried mint (*pudina*)

METHOD

1 Pound the boneless meat on a smooth stone with a wooden mallet. Add meat fat / white butter, 2 ground black cardamoms, ginger powder, and salt. Keep pounding till you get a smooth pulp.

2 Divide the mixture into equal portions and shape into round balls. Keep aside.

3 Boil the bones in 12 cups water for 30 minutes and strain, keep the stock aside.

4 Heat the ghee in a large vessel; add salt, garlic paste, fried onion paste, cloves, cinnamon stick, green cardamom, 1 black cardamom, and bay leaves. Add the stock and keep stirring. Add fennel powder, milk, and whisked yoghurt; mix well. Add the lamb balls called *gushtabas*, one by one, and boil for 30 minutes or till the balls are tender and the gravy is thick. Simmer for about 15 minutes.

5 Sprinkle dried mint and serve hot with steamed rice.

Note: For the diet conscious and those with no time to cook in the traditional way, here are a few tips to make this dish easy.
• *Use a grinder instead of stone and wooden mallet.*
• *Add egg whites instead of meat fat. Or use unsalted butter.*
• *Red meat can be replaced with boneless chicken.*

Rista

LAMB BALLS IN RED GRAVY

Serves: 6

INGREDIENTS

1 kg / 2.2 lb Lamb, boneless, fresh cut from leg
250 gm / 9 oz Meat fat / White butter
10 Bones to make stock
½ cup / 100 gm / 3½ oz Ghee
Salt to taste
2 tsp / 6 gm Red chilli powder
3 Cloves (*laung*)
10 Green cardamoms (*choti elaichi*)
1 tsp / 6 gm Garlic (*lasan*) paste
2 tsp / 6 gm Fried onion paste
2 tsp / 6 gm Turmeric (*haldi*) powder
¼ tsp Saffron (*kesar*)
½ cup Dry cockscomb (*mawal*) extract
  (*see note below*)

METHOD

1 Pound the boneless meat on a smooth stone with a wooden mallet as in *gushtaba*. Add meat fat / white butter while pounding. Make sure the pulp is mixed enough to shape into equal-sized round balls called *ristas*. Keep aside.

2 Boil the bones separately for 30 minutes to make stock.

3 Heat the ghee in large vessel; add, salt, stock, red chilli powder, cloves, green cardamoms, garlic paste, onion paste, and turmeric powder. Keep stirring till the mixture turns red. Add about 15 cups water and bring to the boil.

4 While the gravy is boiling, add the meat balls slowly. Boil for an hour. Add dry cockscomb or saffron extract. Simmer for 5-10 minutes.

5 Serve hot with steamed rice.

*Note: *Mawal (cockscomb) is a dried flower available only in Kashmir. This is generally used for colouring. Mawal extract is made by soaking the flower in 1 cup water for about an hour. Since this may not be easily available, saffron extract is a good substitute. ½ tsp saffron soaked in 1 cup water can be used for this dish.*

Popular Avenue - en route to Gulmarg in the 1930's.

A fisherman casting a net in the Dal lake - home to plenty of fishes. Fishing is the second largest industry in Srinagar and hence the main source of occupation for majority of inhabitants around the lake.

Palak t, Rista

LAMB BALLS COOKED WITH SPINACH

Serves: 6

INGREDIENTS

1 kg / 2.2 lb Minced lamb, mince done as in *Rista*

1 kg / 2.2 lb Spinach (*palak*), washed, boiled, drained

½ cup / 110 ml / 3½ oz Refined oil

3 tsp / 9 gm Red chilli powder

Salt to taste

2 tsp / 6 gm Ginger powder (*sonth*)

2 tsp / 6 gm Turmeric (*haldi*) powder

3 tsp / 9 gm Garlic (*lasan*) paste

2 Cinnamon (*dalchini*) sticks

4 Green cardamoms (*choti elaichi*), crushed

2 tsp / 6 gm Black cardamom (*badi elaichi*) powder

¼ cup Dry cockscomb (*mawal*) extract (see p.39)

1 tsp / 2½ gm Black cumin seeds (*shah jeera*)

METHOD

1 Make round balls of the minced meat weighing 10 gm each.

2 Heat the oil in a deep vessel; add red chilli powder, salt, 8 cups water, ginger powder, turmeric powder, garlic paste, and cinnamon sticks. Bring to the boil. Add lamb balls and cook for 30 minutes on high heat.

3 Squeeze water out of boiled spinach and crush with hands. Add to above mixture; mix well. Add crushed green cardamoms, black cardamom powder and cockscomb extract; cook till the gravy thickens.

4 Serve hot with steamed rice.

Kashmiri hindu pandits in the 1890's.

Kabargah

FRIED BREASTS OF LAMB

Serves: 6

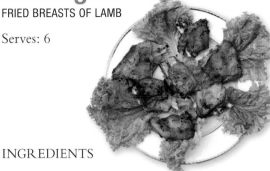

INGREDIENTS

1 kg / 2.2 lb Breast of Lamb, cut into square /
   rectangle pieces, washed
3 cups / 750 ml / 24 fl oz Water
3 cups / 720 ml / 23 fl oz Milk
2 Bay leaves (*tej patta*)
2 Cloves (*laung*)
2 Cinnamon (*dalchini*) sticks
2 Black cardamoms (*badi elaichi*)
5 Green cardamoms (*choti elaichi*)
1 tsp / 3 gm Cumin (*jeera*) powder
½ tsp / 1½ gm Ginger powder (*sonth*)
½ tsp / 1½ gm Fennel (*saunf*) powder
Salt to taste
½ tsp Saffron (*kesar*)
1 cup / 220 ml / 7 fl oz Ghee / Refined oil
2 portions Silver leaves (*varq*) (optional)

METHOD

1 Cook the meat in a deep vessel. Add water,
   milk, and all the ingredients except oil. Cover
   and cook till the meat is tender.

2 Remove the lid and check if the meat is tender.
   Boil till the gravy is absorbed and the meat is
   tender.

3 Remove the meat pieces, one by one, with a
   tong so that they don't break. Separate them in
   a large plate.

4 Heat the oil in pan; fry the meat, 2-3 pieces at
   a time, until light brown.

5 Serve hot as a snack or with main course

Aab Gosht

LAMB IN MILK GRAVY

Serves: 6

INGREDIENTS

1 kg / 2.2 lb Lamb, cut from shoulder, washed
½ cup / 110 ml / 3½ oz Refined oil
3 Cloves (*laung*)
5 Green cardamoms (*choti elaichi*), crushed
3 tsp / 9 gm Fennel (*saunf*) powder
2 tsp / 12 gm Fried onion paste
2 tsp / 12 gm Garlic (*lasan*) paste
3 cups / 720 ml / 23 fl oz Full-cream milk,
   boiled
Salt to taste

METHOD

1 Add 8 cups water in a deep vessel and boil the
   lamb for 5 minutes. Drain the stock in another pot.

2 Wash lamb in cold water and add to the stock.

3 Heat the oil in a pressure cooker; add cloves, lamb
   with stock, green cardamoms, fennel powder,
   fried onion paste, and garlic paste. Pressure cook
   for 5 minutes. Open the lid when the pressure
   drops to check if the meat is tender.

4 Add milk and mix well. Boil till the gravy is thick.

Embroiderers at work. Designs such as the paisley motifs, lotuses, chinar leaves, birds and flowers are stitched by hand in fine silk threads on woollen garments and shawls.

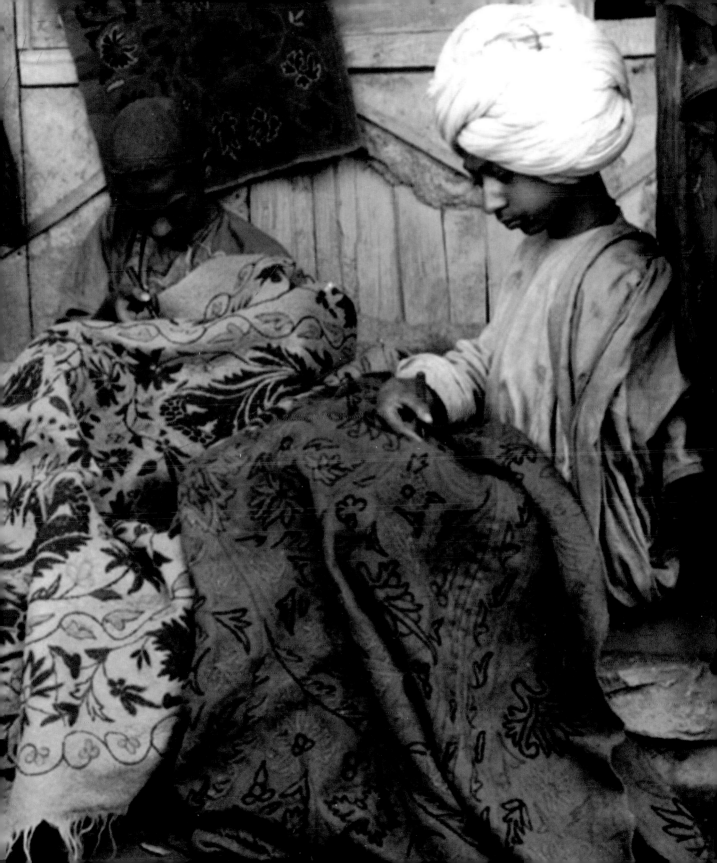

Dhaniwal Korma

LAMB IN CORIANDER FLAVOURED GRAVY

Serves: 6

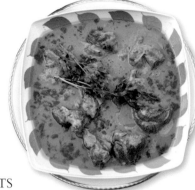

INGREDIENTS

1 kg / 2.2 lb Lamb, cut from leg, washed
1 cup / 220 ml / 7 fl oz Refined oil
3 Cloves (*laung*)
3 tbsp Fried onion paste
1 tsp / 6 gm Garlic (*lasan*) paste
Salt to taste
6 Green cardamoms (*choti elaichi*), crushed
1 tsp / 3 gm Turmeric (*haldi*) powder
2 tsp / 6 gm Coriander (*dhaniya*) powder
½ tsp Saffron (*kesar*) extract
2 cups / 450 gm / 1 lb Yoghurt (*dahi*), whisked
½ cup / 30 gm / 1 oz Green coriander (*hara dhaniya*), chopped

METHOD

1 Boil the lamb in a deep vessel for 5 minutes; drain the stock and keep aside.

2 Wash the lamb in cold water and keep aside.

3 Heat the oil in a pressure cooker; add the cloves, onion paste, garlic paste, salt, green cardamoms, and the lamb; mix well. Add the stock, turmeric powder, coriander powder, and saffron extract; pressure cook for 5 minutes.

4 When the pressure drops, check if the lamb is tender. Add yoghurt and mix well with a ladle. Cook on high flame till the gravy thickens.

5 Serve hot garnished with green coriander.

Alubukhar Korma

LAMB COOKED WITH PLUMS

Serves: 6

INGREDIENTS

1 kg / 2.2 lb Lamb, boneless, cut from leg
1 cup Dried plums (*alubukhara*), washed and soaked
1 cup / 220 ml / 7 oz Refined oil
3 Cloves (*laung*)
Salt to taste
2 Cinnamon (*dalchini*) sticks
6 Green cardamoms (*choti elaichi*), crushed
3 tsp / 9 gm Red chilli powder
1 tsp / 3 gm Turmeric (*haldi*) powder
½ cup / 100 ml / 3½ fl oz Tamarind (*imli*) liquid
1 tsp / 6 gm Garlic paste

METHOD

1 Heat the oil in a pressure cooker; add the lamb, cloves, salt, cinnamon sticks, and green cardamoms. Fry till golden brown.

2 Add red chilli powder, turmeric powder, and 6 cups water; pressure cook for 10 minutes.

3 Open the lid when the pressure drops and add the dried plums and tamarind liquid; cook till the gravy thickens. Mix well and cook on low heat till the plum is soft.

4 Serve hot with boiled rice.

Palak t, Syun

SPINACH COOKED WITH LAMB

Serves: 6

INGREDIENTS

1 kg / 2.2 lb Lamb, boneless, preferably
2 kg / 4.4 lb Spinach (*palak*), stems removed,
  cleaned, washed thoroughly
1 cup / 220 ml / 7 fl oz Mustard oil
Salt to taste
½ tsp Asafoetida (*hing*)
500 gm / 1.1 lb Tomatoes, chopped
4 tsp / 12 gm Red chilli powder
2 tsp / 6 gm Ginger powder (*sonth*)
2 tsp / 6 gm Cumin (*jeera*) powder

METHOD

1 Boil the spinach in 6 cups water till tender.
  Remove, drain and mash with hands.

2 Heat the oil in a pressure cooker; add salt,
  asafoetida, and lamb with 1 cup water and
  pressure cook for 10 minutes. Add tomatoes
  and keep frying till the tomatoes are mashed.

3 Add the mashed spinach and keep stirring on
  high flame. Add red chilli powder, ginger
  powder, and cumin powder; mix well. Add
  ½ cup water and bring the mixture to the boil.
  Cook till the gravy is dry. Serve with rice or
  chapatti.

Gole al Syun

PUMPKIN COOKED WITH LAMB

Serves: 6

INGREDIENTS

1 kg / 2.2 lb Lamb, cut from leg, washed
1 kg / 2.2 lb Pumpkin (*kaddu*), peeled, washed,
  cut into medium-sized cubes
½ cup / 110 ml / 3½ fl oz Mustard / Refined oil
Salt to taste
¼ tsp Asafoetida (*hing*)
1 tsp / 3 gm Turmeric (*haldi*) powder
1 tsp / 3 gm Ginger powder (*sonth*)
2 tsp / 6 gm Fennel (*saunf*) powder
4 Dried red chillies (*sookhi lal mirch*)

METHOD

1 Heat the oil in a pressure cooker; add salt,
  asafoetida, and meat. Fry till the water is dried
  up. Add 1 cup water and pressure cook for
  5 minutes.

2 Open the lid when the pressure drops and if
  meat is half tender, add pumpkin cubes and
  the spice powders. Pressure cook for 5 minutes
  more. Remove the lid and transfer into a
  serving bowl.

3 Serve garnished with dried red chillies and
  enjoy with chapatti, rice or *nan*.

Kaliya

LAMB IN YELLOW GRAVY

Serves: 6

INGREDIENTS

1 kg / 2.2 lb
  Lamb, cut from
  shoulder and
  breast, washed
2 tbsp / 30 ml /
  1 fl oz Mustard /
  Refined oil
2 Cloves (*laung*)
2 Bay leaves (*tej patta*)
¼ tsp Asafoetida (*hing*)
2 tsp / 6 gm Turmeric (*haldi*) powder
2 tsp / 6 gm Ginger powder (*sonth*)
3 tsp / 9 gm Fennel (*saunf*) powder
Salt to taste
½ cup / 120 ml / 4 fl oz Milk
1 tsp / 3 gm Cumin (*jeera*) powder
1 tsp / 3 gm Black cardamoms (*badi elaichi*),
  coarsely ground
3 Green cardamoms (*choti elaichi*), crushed

METHOD

1 Heat the oil in pressure cooker; add cloves, bay
  leaves, asafoetida, and meat. Fry for 10 minutes.
  Add 6 cups water, turmeric powder, ginger
  powder, fennel powder, and salt. Pressure cook
  for 5-10 minutes.

2 Remove the lid of the pressure cooker and
  check if the meat is tender. Add milk, cumin
  powder, black cardamom and green cardamom
  powder; bring to the boil. Simmer for
  5 minutes.

3 Serve with rice.

Note: This is an excellent dish for the old and young. Earlier, kaliya was cooked in a clay degchi for hours on a slow fire. Today, although a pressure cooker is used, at traditional weddings it is still cooked in degchis. This dish is still popular at Kashmiri Pandit weddings.

Rogan Josh

LAMB IN RED GRAVY

Serves: 6

INGREDIENTS

1 kg / 2.2 lb Lamb,
  cut from leg,
  washed
1 cup / 220 ml / 7 fl oz
  Mustard / Refined oil
Salt to taste
¼ tsp Asafoetida (*hing*)
2 Cinnamon (*dalchini*) sticks
2 Bay leaves (*tej patta*)
2 Cloves (*laung*)
1 tsp / 2 gm Cumin (*jeera*) seeds
3 tsp / 6 gm Red chilli powder
½ cup / 110 gm / 3½ oz Yoghurt (*dahi*)
2 tsp / 6 gm Ginger powder (*sonth*)
3 tsp / 9 gm Fennel (*saunf*) powder
3 Black cardamoms (*badi elaichi*), crushed
3 Green cardamoms (*choti elaichi*), crushed
1 tsp / 3 gm Cumin powder
¼ Saffron (*kesar*), optional

METHOD

1 Heat the oil in a vessel; add salt, asafoetida,
  cinnamon sticks, bay leaves, cloves, cumin
  seeds, and meat. Fry till the meat turns brown.

2 Add 1 cup water and red chilli powder; keep
  stirring with a ladle till the colour turns red.

3 Whisk yoghurt and add to the meat. Add
  2 cups water, ginger powder and fennel powder;
  cook till the meat is tender.

4 Add the cardamoms and cumin powder; mix
  well. Finally, add saffron if using. Simmer for 2
  minutes and serve with steamed rice.

Note: Cook in a pressure cooker, if in a hurry. Personally I do not use a pressure cooker if the quality of meat is good, as it gets tender while frying.

Gogji t, Syun

LAMB WITH TURNIPS

Serves: 6

INGREDIENTS

1 kg / 2.2 lb
  Lamb, cut from
  breast and shoulder,
  washed
500 gm / 1.1 lb Turnips
  (*shalgam*), peeled, cut into 4 pieces
½ cup / 110 ml / 3½ fl oz Mustard oil
2 Cloves (*laung*)
Salt to taste
½ tsp Asafoetida (*hing*)
2 tsp / 6 gm Turmeric (*haldi*) powder
3 tsp / 9 gm Fennel (*saunf*) powder
2 tsp / 6 gm Ginger powder (*sonth*)

METHOD

1 Heat the oil in a pressure cooker; add cloves, meat, salt, and asafoetida. Keep frying for 10 minutes. Pour 6 cups water, turmeric powder, fennel powder, and ginger powder; mix well. Pressure cook for 5 minutes; remove from heat.

2 Heat 2 tbsp oil in a frying pan; fry the turnips 4-5 pieces at a time.

3 Remove the lid of the cooker, add the fried turnips and pressure cook again for 2 minutes. Remove from heat and let it cool down.

4 Remove the lid when the pressure drops and check if the meat is tender, if you find the gravy is thin then boil on high flame till the gravy thickens.

5 Serve hot.

Vost Haak t, Syun

GREEN / RED LEAVES WITH LAMB

Serves: 6

INGREDIENTS

1 kg / 2.2 lb Lamb,
  boneless, cut from
  leg, washed
500 gm / 1.1 lb *Vost
  haak*, sorted, washed,
  drained
1 cup / 220 ml / 7 fl oz Mustard / Refined oil
Salt to taste
½ tsp Asafoetida (*hing*)
2 Cloves (*laung*)
1 tsp / 2 gm Cumin (*jeera*) seeds
3 tsp / 9 gm Red chilli powder
2 tsp / 6 gm Ginger powder (*sonth*)
3 tsp / 9 gm Fennel (*saunf*) powder
1 cup / 225 gm / 8 oz Yoghurt (*dahi*), whisked
2 tsp / 6 gm Cumin (*jeera*) powder

METHOD

1 Heat the oil in a pressure cooker; add salt, asafoetida, cloves, cumin seeds, and lamb. Fry till the lamb is golden brown.

2 Add *vost haak*; mix well. Add red chilli powder, ginger powder, fennel powder, and 4 cups water; mix well with a ladle and pressure cook for 10 minutes.

3 Open the lid and check if the meat is tender. Add yoghurt and cook on high heat, stirring till the lamb and *vost haak* are really mixed well.

4 Serve hot.

Note: Vost haak is a speciality of Kashmir. It is generally available in spring, the leaves are red or green. It is available in Delhi in winters from November onwards and if you do not get vost haak *you can make* cholai ka sag *instead.*

Ther VVIP boat on the Jhelum River in the early 1900's.

Oluv t, Syun

POTATOES AND LAMB IN THICK GRAVY

Serves: 6

INGREDIENTS

1 kg / 2.2 lb Lamb, cut from leg
500 gm / 1.1 lb Potatoes, peeled, washed, cut into 4 long pieces
1 cup / 220 ml / 7 fl oz Mustard oil
2 Bay leaves (*tej patta*)
2 Cloves (*laung*)
1 Cinnamon (*dalchini*) stick
Salt to taste
3 tsp / 9 gm Red chilli powder
½ tsp Asafoetida (*hing*)
2 tsp / 6 gm Ginger powder (*sonth*)
3 tsp / 9 gm Fennel (*saunf*) powder
2 tsp / 6 gm Cumin (*jeera*) powder
3 Black cardamoms (*badi elaichi*), coarsely ground

METHOD

1 Heat the oil in a pan; fry the potatoes till they turn brown. Keep aside.

2 Reheat the same oil in a pressure cooker; add meat, bay leaves, cloves, cinnamon stick, and salt. Fry till the meat is golden brown.

3 Pour ½ cup water and red chilli powder; stir till the mixture turns red. Pour 6 cups water and all the spice powders. Pressure cook for 2 minutes. Remove the lid and check if the meat is tender. Then add fried potatoes and boil for 5-8 minutes. Add black cardamom powder and mix well.

4 Serve hot with steamed rice or chapatti.

Champ

LAMB CHOPS

Serves: 6

INGREDIENTS

1 kg / 2.2 lb Lamb chops, flattened nicely
1 cup / 225 gm / 8 oz Yoghurt (*dahi*)
2 tsp / 6 gm Ginger (*adrak*) paste, fresh
2 tsp / 6 gm Garlic (*lasan*) paste
Salt to taste
1 tbsp / 15 ml Lemon (*nimbu*) juice
2 tsp / 10 gm Papaya paste
3 tbsp / 45 ml / 1½ fl oz Refined oil for mixing
1 tsp / 5 ml Wine vinegar
2 tsp / 6 gm Red chilli powder
2 tsp / 6 gm Cumin (*jeera*) powder
1 cup / 220 ml / 7 fl oz Refined oil for frying

METHOD

1 Mix the lamb chops, yoghurt, ginger paste, garlic paste, salt, lemon juice, papaya paste, oil, vinegar, red chilli powder, and cumin powder together in a bowl. Marinate for 12 hours.

2 Heat the oil in a frying pan; fry the chops till golden brown. Alternatively preheat oven to 180°C / 350°F and grill.

3 Serve hot with *nan* or chapatti or rice pulao.

Note: When buying lamb chops make sure you get them chopped nicely. They should be flatted nicely.

Bukvetch Chagil t, Charvan

SPICY KIDNEYS, TESTES AND LIVER

Serves: 6

INGREDIENTS

1 kg / 2.2 lb Lamb liver, testes, kidney washed
  and cut into 4 pieces, removing fat from kidney
1 cup / 220 ml / 7 fl oz Mustard / Refined oil
2 Cloves (*laung*)
Salt to taste
½ tsp Asafoetida (*hing*)
3 tsp / 9 gm Red chilli powder
2 tsp / 6 gm Ginger powder (*sonth*)
1 tsp / 3 gm Turmeric (*haldi*) powder
2 tsp / 6 gm Fennel (*saunf*) powder
1 tsp / 3 gm Cumin (*jeera*) powder

METHOD

1 Heat the oil in a frying pan; add cloves, salt,
   asafoetida, liver and kidneys. Fry till golden
   brown. Add red chilli powder and ½ cup water;
   mix well. Add all the spice powders and 2 cups
   water. Cook till the liver is tender.

2 In a separate pot, boil the testes in 2 cups water
   with ½ tsp turmeric powder and ½ tsp salt for
   3 minutes. Drain and add to the liver. Bring to
   the boil and serve with rice, chapatti, *nan* or
   tandoori roti.

Tchokh Charvan

TANGY LIVER

Serves 6

INGREDIENTS

1 kg / 2.2 lb Liver, cut into small cubes, 1 cm
  long x ½ cm wide
½ cup / 110 ml / 3½ fl oz Mustard oil
2 Cloves (*laung*)
¼ tsp Asafoetida (*hing*)
3 tsp / 9 gm Red chilli powder
2 tsp / 6 gm Ginger powder (*sonth*)
2 tsp / 6 gm Fennel (*saunf*) powder
1 tsp / 3 gm Turmeric (*haldi*) powder
½ cup / 100 ml / 3½ fl oz Tamarind (*imli*) liquid
1 tsp / 3 gm Cumin (*jeera*) powder
Salt to taste

METHOD

1 Heat the oil in a pot; add cloves, asafoetida, and
   liver. Fry till brown. Pour 2 cups water, red
   chilli powder, ginger powder, fennel powder,
   turmeric powder, and salt; cook for 10 minutes.

2 Add tamarind liquid and boil for 5 minutes.
   Reduce heat and simmer for 5 minutes. Add
   cumin powder; mix well.

3 Serve hot with rice.

Pachh Rogan Josh

TROTTER IN RED GRAVY

Serves: 6

INGREDIENTS

12 Trotters, cleaned,
    trimmed and washed in hot water
2 cups / 440 ml / 15 fl oz Mustard oil
½ tsp Asafoetida (*hing*)
Salt to taste
1 tsp / 2 gm Cumin (*jeera*) seeds
2 Cloves (*laung*)
2 Cinnamon (*dalchini*) sticks
1 tsp / 2 gm Red chilli powder
3 tsp / 9 gm Fennel (*saunf*) powder
2 tsp / 6 gm Ginger powder (*sonth*)
2 tsp / 6 gm Cumin (*jeera*) powder
2 Green cardamoms (*choti elaichi*), crushed
2 Black cardamoms (*badi elaichi*), crushed

METHOD

1 Heat the oil a pressure cooker; add asafoetida, salt, cumin seeds, cloves, cinnamon sticks, and trotters. Fry till golden brown. Add red chilli powder and 6 cups water; mix. And rest of the spice powders.

2 Pressure cook for 30 minutes. Open the lid when the pressure drops and check if the trotters are tender, if not pressure cook again for 15 minutes and keep checking till they are tender.

3 Add crushed green and black cardamoms; cook till oil separates.

4 Serve hot with steamed rice

Facing page: Through the blooming mustard fields near Srinagar.
Photograph: Mukhtar Ahmad

Pachh Ras

TROTTER SOUP

Serves: 6

INGREDIENTS

10 Sheep knuckles, washed in hot water
2 tbsp / 30 ml / 1 fl oz Mustard oil
¼ tsp Asafoetida (*hing*)
3 tsp / 9 gm Fennel (*saunf*) powder
2 tsp / 6 gm Ginger powder (*sonth*)
2 tsp / 6 gm Turmeric (*haldi*) powder
2 Black cardamoms (*badi elaichi*)
Salt to taste

METHOD

1 Cook the knuckles in a pressure cooker with 20 cups water and all the spices for about 30 minutes.

2 Remove the lid when the pressure drops and check if they are tender. If not, cook for some more time till they are tender.

3 You can remove the knuckles and serve the soup only, or enjoy the whole dish with steamed rice.

Note: In olden times this soup was cooked in handies on slow heat the whole day. Today we can use a pressure cooker. So enjoy the soup which is an excellent source of calcium. Get knuckles trimmed and cleaned from the butcher.

A shikara ride in the pristine Dal Lake.
Photograph: Wajid Dabru

Chicken & Fish

Kokur Masala

CHICKEN MASALA

Serves: 6

INGREDIENTS

1 kg / 2.2 lb Chicken, thigh and leg pieces, washed
2 cups / 440 ml / 15 fl oz Refined oil
2 Bay leaves (*tej patta*)
2 Cinnamon (*dalchini*) sticks
3 Cloves (*laung*)
1 cup Onions, chopped
500 gm / 1.1 lb Tomatoes, chopped
3 tsp / 9 gm Red chilli powder
3 tsp / 9 gm Cumin (*jeera*) powder
Salt to taste
6 Green cardamoms (*choti elaichi*), coarsely ground
2 Black cardamoms (*badi elaichi*), coarsely ground
5 Eggs, hard-boiled for decoration

METHOD

1 Heat the oil in a frying pan; fry the chicken, 4-5 pieces at a time, until brown.

2 Heat 2 tbsp oil in a separate vessel; add bay leaves, cinnamon sticks, cloves, and onions. Fry till light brown. Add tomatoes and keep stirring till you get a paste. Add red chilli powder, cumin powder, salt, and 1 cup water. Cook till the water is dry.

3 Add fried chicken and mix well. Cook on very low heat for 30 minutes, keep checking to prevent burning. Sprinkle green and black cardamom powder and mix well.

4 Garnish with boiled eggs, cut into half and serve with *nan* or tandoori roti or rice.

Kokur t, Nadir

CHICKEN AND LOTUS STEMS

Serves: 6

INGREDIENTS

1 kg / 2.2 lb Chicken, washed
500 gm / 1.1 lb Lotus stems (*kamal kakri*), washed, cut into 3″-long pieces
2 cups / 440 ml / 15 fl oz Mustard / Refined oil
Salt to taste
½ tsp Asafoetida (*hing*)
2 Cloves (*laung*)
2 Cinnamon (*dalchini*) sticks
3 tsp / 9 gm Red chilli powder
2 tsp / 6 gm Ginger powder (*sonth*)
3 tsp / 9 gm Fennel (*saunf*) powder
3 tsp / 9 gm Cumin (*jeera*) powder
3 Black cardamoms (*badi elaichi*), coarsely ground

METHOD

1 Heat the oil in a frying pan; fry the lotus stems till golden brown.

2 Take the already hot oil in a deep vessel; add chicken, salt, asafoetida, cloves, and cinnamon sticks. Fry the chicken till golden brown.

3 Add red chilli powder, 4 cups water, and all the powdered spices. Add fried lotus stems and bring the mixture to the boil for 5-10 minutes. Simmer for 5 minutes. Add black cardamom powder.

4 Serve hot.

Kokur Yakhni

CHICKEN IN YOGHURT

Serves: 6

INGREDIENTS

1 kg / 2.2 lb Chicken,
   breasts and leg pieces,
   washed
½ cup / 110 ml / 3½ fl oz
Salt to taste
1¼ tsp Asafoetida (*hing*)
2 Bay leaves (*tej patta*)
3 Cinnamon (*dalchini*) sticks
3 Cloves (*laung*)
1 tsp / 2 gm Cumin (*jeera*) seeds
3 tsp / 9 gm Fennel (*saunf*) powder
2 tsp / 6 gm Ginger powder (*sonth*)
2 cups / 450 gm / 1 lb Yoghurt (*dahi*)
2 Black cardamoms (*badi elaichi*), coarsely ground
   (skin on)
5 Green cardamoms (*choti elaichi*), coarsely
   ground with the skin
2 tsp / 5 gm Black cumin (*shah jeera*) seeds

METHOD

1 Heat the oil in a deep vessel; add salt, asafoetida,
   bay leaves, cinnamon sticks, cloves, cumin seeds
   and chicken. Fry for 10 minutes. Pour 4 cups
   water and all the spice powders; cook till the
   chicken is tender.

2 Whisk yoghurt in a bowl. Add to the chicken
   mixture; mixing well. Bring to the boil for 5
   minutes.

3 Add ground black and green cardamoms; mix
   well.

4 Serve hot with steamed rice, chapatti, or any
   bread of your choice.

*Note: Lamb yakhni is also cooked similarly. This dish should
be eaten with Phool Rogenjosh (see p.88) or Palak t, Nadir
(see p.74).*

Top: An Englishman enjoying a tonga ride.
Bottom: On the banks of the River Jhelum.

Gaad t, Tamater

FISH IN TOMATO GRAVY

Serves: 6

INGREDIENTS

1 kg / 2.2 lb Fish (*Singhara/Salmon/Rohu*),
    cleaned, trimmed, cut into 2″-thick round
    pieces
1 cup Tomatoes, chopped
½ tsp / 1½ gm Turmeric (*haldi*) powder
1 cup / 220 ml / 7 fl oz Mustard oil for frying
Salt to taste
½ tsp Asafoetida (*hing*)
2 Cloves (*laung*)
2 tsp / 6 gm Red chilli powder
2 tsp / 6 gm Fennel (*saunf*) powder
2 tsp / 6 gm Ginger powder (*sonth*)
1 tsp / 3 gm *Ver* masala (see p. 16)

METHOD

1 Wash fish and drain in a holed basket. Sprinkle
   turmeric powder all over.

2 Heat the oil in a frying pan; sprinkle a pinch of
   salt over the fish to avoid splattering. Fry the
   fish till brown, turning it once or twice, over
   high heat.

3 Take the leftover oil in a separate vessel; add
   asafoetida, cloves, and tomatoes. Pour ½ cup
   water and make a paste.

4 Add all the spices with 4 cups water. Bring to
   the boil. Add fried fish and cook till the gravy
   thickens.

5 Serve with steamed rice.

Gaad t, Nadir

FISH COOKED WITH LOTUS STEMS

Serves: 6

INGREDIENTS

1 kg / 2.2 lb Fish, cleaned, trimmed, cut into
    cubes
500 gm / 1.1 lb Lotus stems (*kamal kakri*),
    washed, cut into 3 cm pieces
1 tsp / 3 gm Turmeric (*haldi*) powder
1 cup / 220 ml / 7 fl oz Mustard oil
½ tsp Asafoetida (*hing*) liquid (see p. 17)
Salt to taste
3 tsp / 9 gm Red chilli powder
2 Cloves (*laung*)
3 tsp / 9 gm Fennel (*saunf*) powder
2 tsp / 6 gm Ginger powder (*sonth*)
2 tbsp / 30 ml / 1 fl oz Tamarind (*imli*) liquid or
2 tbsp / 10 ml Lemon (*nimbu*) juice
2 tsp / 6 gm *Ver* masala (see p. 16)

METHOD

1 Wash the fish, drain and sprinkle turmeric
   powder all over.

2 Heat the oil in a frying pan; fry the lotus stems
   till light brown. Keep aside.

3 Fry the fish in the same oil till golden brown.

4 Take the same oil in another vessel; add,
   asafoetida liquid, salt, red chilli powder,
   cloves, and 2 cups water. Bring to the boil and
   stir till the mixture turns red. Add 4 more
   cups of water, fennel powder, ginger powder,
   fried fish, and lotus stems; cook for 10-15
   minutes. Add ¼ cup
   tamarind liquid or
   lemon juice and *ver*
   masala; cook for
   5 more minutes.

5 Serve hot with
   steamed rice.

Gaad t, Munj

FISH COOKED WITH KNOL KHOL

Serves: 6

INGREDIENTS

1 kg / 2.2 lb Fish (*Singhara/Salmon/Rohu*),
cleaned, trimmed, cut into 2-thick round
pieces
500 gm / 1.1 lb Knol khol (*kholrabi*), peeled, cut
into 2″- thick round pieces
1 tsp / 3 gm Turmeric (*haldi*) powder
1 cup / 220 ml / 7 fl oz Mustard oil
2 Cloves (*laung*)
½ tsp Asafoetida (*hing*) liquid (see p. 17)
3 tsp / 9 gm Red chilli powder
Salt to taste
2 tsp / 6 gm Ginger powder (*sonth*)
3 tsp / 9 gm Fennel (*saunf*) powder
2 tsp / 6 gm *Ver* masala (see p. 16)

METHOD

1 Wash the fish, sprinkle turmeric powder and
keep aside to drain in a big holed basket.

2 Heat the oil in a frying pan; fry the fish till
golden brown.

3 Fry knol khol in the same oil till golden brown.

4 Take the same oil in another vessel; add
cloves, asafoetida liquid, red chilli powder,
salt, ginger powder, and fennel powder. Add
4 cups water and bring to the boil. Add fried
fish and knol khol; cook till the gravy
thickens and fish is tender.

5 Sprinkle
ver masala and
cook for a
minute.
Serve with
steamed
rice.

Gaad t, Muj

FISH COOKED WITH RADISH

Serves: 6

INGREDIENTS

1 kg / 2.2 lb Fish
(*Singhara/Salmon/Rohu*),
cleaned, trimmed, cut into
2″-thick, round pieces
500 gm / 1.1 lb Radish (*shalgam*), peeled, washed,
cut into 2″-thick, round pieces
1 cup / 220 ml / 7 fl oz Mustard oil
Salt to taste
½ tsp Asafoetida (*hing*)
3 tsp / 9 gm Red chilli powder
3 tsp / 9 gm Fennel (*saunf*) powder
2 tsp / 6 gm Ginger powder (*sonth*)
1 tsp / 3 gm Turmeric (*haldi*) powder
2 tsp / 6 gm *Ver* masala (see p. 16)
¼ cup / 50 ml / 1¾ fl oz Tamarind (*imli*) liquid
3 tbsp / 45 ml / 1½ fl oz Lemon (*nimbu*) juice

METHOD

1 Wash and drain the fish. Sprinkle turmeric
powder over the fish.

2 Heat the oil in a frying pan; fry the fish golden
brown. Keep aside. Fry the radish in the same
oil and keep aside.

3 Take the leftover oil in a deep vessel; add salt,
asafoetida, red chilli powder, 6 cups water, add
all the spice powders; bring to the boil. Add fish
and radish and cook till the gravy thickens.

4 Lastly pour the tamarind liquid or lemon juice
and boil for a minute.

5 Serve with steamed rice.

One of the most unique features of Srinagar was the prevelance of wooden architecture. Seen here is a bridge made of deodar on the river Jhelum .

Gaad t, Choont

FISH COOKED WITH GREEN APPLES

Serves: 6

INGREDIENTS

1 kg / 2.2 lb Fish (*Singhara/Salmon/ Rohu*), cleaned, trimmed, cut into 2″-thick, round pieces
500 gm / 1.1 lb Cooking green apples, cut into 4 pieces each
1 tsp / 3 gm Turmeric (*haldi*) powder
1 cup / 220 ml / 7 fl oz Mustard oil
2 Cloves (*laung*)
½ tsp Asafoetida (*hing*)
3 tsp / 9 gm Red chilli powder
2 tsp / 6 gm Ginger powder (*sonth*)
2 tsp / 6 gm Fennel (*saunf*) powder
Salt to taste
4 Green chillies

METHOD

1 Wash and drain the fish. Sprinkle turmeric powder and keep aside for some time till the water is drained out.

2 Heat the oil in a pan; fry the fish till golden brown.

3 Fry the apples in the same oil turning once; remove and keep aside.

4 Take the leftover oil in a separate pan; add cloves, asafoetida, red chilli powder, 6 cups water and rest of the spice powders. Add fish and cook for 10 minutes. Add fried apples and cook for another 5 minutes.

5 Serve hot garnished with green chillies and accompanied with rice.

Gaad t, Aar

FISH COOKED WITH PLUM

Serves: 6

INGREDIENTS

1 kg / 2.2 lb Fish (*Singhara/Salmon/Rohu*), cleaned, trimmed, cut into 2-thick, round pieces
500 gm / 1.1 lb Raw plum, washed, pat dried, pricked with a knife
1 tsp / 3 gm Turmeric (*haldi*) powder
1 cup / 220 ml / 7 oz Mustard oil
Salt to taste
½ tsp Asafoetida (*hing*)
3 tsp / 9 gm Red chilli powder
2 tsp / 6 gm Ginger powder (*sonth*)
2 tsp / 6 gm Fennel (*saunf*) powder

METHOD

1 Wash the fish and drain in a holed basket. Sprinkle turmeric powder all over the fish.

2 Heat the oil in a frying pan; add a little bit of salt and fry the fish till golden brown.

3 Take the leftover oil in a large vessel; add asafoetida, salt, 6 cups water, red chilli powder, and rest of the spice powders; bring to the boil. Add fish and cook for 15 minutes. Add plum and cook for 5 minutes on high heat.

4 Serve hot with steamed rice.

Haak t, Thool

GREENS WITH EGGS

Serves: 6

INGREDIENTS

10 Eggs, hard-boiled, shelled
500 gm / 1.1 lb Kashmiri greens (*haak*), cleaned, washed
1 cup / 220 ml / 7 fl oz Mustard oil for frying
½ tsp Asafoetida (*hing*)
Salt to taste
3 tsp / 9 gm Red chilli powder
2 tsp / 6 gm Ginger powder (*sonth*)
5 Dried red chillies (*sookhi lal mirch*), deseeded
2 tsp / 6 gm *Ver* masala (see p. 16)

METHOD

1 Prick the eggs with a tooth pick and keep aside.

2 Heat the oil in a deep pan; fry the eggs, 4-5 at a time, till light brown.

3 Take the leftover oil in a pressure cooker; add asafoetida, salt red chilli powder, ginger powder, 6 cups water, eggs, and greens. Pressure cook for 10 minutes or till 2 whistles. Remove from heat.

4 Open the lid when the pressure drops. Add dried red chillies and *ver* masala. Return to heat and cook on high heat, till the gravy thickens.

5 Serve hot with rice or chapatti.

HoGaad t, Haak

DRIED FISH COOKED WITH GREENS

Serves: 6

INGREDIENTS

250 gm / 9 oz Dried fish, skin scraped, fins removed, soaked for 5 minutes
200 gm / 7 oz Kashmiri spinach (*haak*), cleaned, washed
½ cup / 110 ml / 3½ fl oz Mustard oil
½ tsp Asafoetida (*hing*)
2 tsp / 6 gm Red chilli powder
1 tsp / 3 gm Ginger powder (*sonth*)
1 tsp / 3 gm Turmeric (*haldi*) powder
1 tsp / 3 gm Fennel (*saunf*) powder
Salt to taste
4 Dried red chillies (*sookhi lal mirch*), deseeded
1 tsp / 3 gm *Ver* masala (see p. 16)

METHOD

1 Scrape the fish skin again and wash till really clean. Drain. Cut into 4 pieces if they are large and if small leave the fish whole.

2 Heat the oil in a deep pot, add asafoetida, salt, and fish. Fry till dark brown (do not burn). Add red chilli powder, 4 cups water, ginger powder, turmeric powder, and fennel powder; bring to the boil.

3 Add *haak* and cook till the fish and greens are tender. Add dried red chillies and *ver* masala; cook for 2 minutes. Serve hot.

Note: Dried fish is available in Srinagar. Small fish called sardine is sun-dried in summer to be used in winters. This sun-dried fish is called Raz *hogard. The larger ones are cleaned after slitting their stomachs and are called* Pach *hogard.*

A view of the snow-capped mountains and the
blooming mustard field
Photograph: S. Irfan

Top: A papier mâché worker.
Bottom: Quiet waters: serene and beautiful!

VEGETARIAN

75 **SOUCHAL T NADIR**
Greens with fried lotus stems

78 **TAMATAR T, NADIR**
Lotus stems cooked with tomatoes

79 **TCHOK NADIR**
Lotus stems in sour gravy

79 **VOST HAAK T NADIR**
Red coloured greens with lotus stems

80 **NADIR YAKHNI**
Lotus stems in yoghurt

81 **WANGEN YAKHNI**
Fried aubergine in yoghurt

82 **RAZMA HEMB T, WANGEN**
French beans with aubergine

82 **TCHONT T WANGEN**
Cooking apples with aubergine

83 **SOUCHAL T WANGEN**
Kashmiri spinach with aubergine

83 **TAMATER T, WANGEN**
Tomatoes with aubergine

86 **TCHOK WANGEN**
Tangy aubergine

86 **AL ROGAN JOSH**
Pumpkin in red gravy

87 **AL YAKHNI**
Bottle gourd in yoghurt

88 **KANGUCH YAKHNI**
Mushrooms in yoghurt sauce

88 **PHOOL ROGAN JOSH**
Cauliflower in thick red gravy

89 **KANGUCH T, CHAMAN**
Mushrooms and cottage cheese in yoghurt

89 **CHAMAN T MEETH**
Cottage cheese in fenugreek sauce

91 **CHAMAN KALIYA**
Cottage cheese in yellow gravy

92 **WANGEN HETCH, TAMBER LAGITH**
Dried aubergine in tamarind sauce

92 **AL HETCH IN ZAMUDUD**
Dried bottle gourd in yoghurt

93 **HAAK T CHAMAN**
Kashmiri spinach with cottage cheese

93 **THOOL RAZMA YAKHNI**
Green kidney beans in yoghurt

94 **KAREL T WANGEN DUED LAGITH**
Bitter gourd and aubergine in yoghurt

95 **GURDOL T, OLUV**
Raw plum with potatoes

95 **VERIFOL T, OLUV**
Sun-dried black lentils with potatoes

96 **AL KANEJ T, WANGEN**
Pumpkin greens with aubergine

96 **MUJ PATTAR T, WANGEN**
Radish leaves with aubergine

Munj Haak

KNOL KHOL FLAVOURED WITH ASAFOETIDA

Serves: 6

INGREDIENTS

1 kg / 2.2 lb Knol khol (*kholrabi*) with leaves,
    medium-sized, peeled
½ cup / 110 ml / 3½ fl oz Mustard oil
Salt to taste
½ tsp Asafoetida (*hing*)
6 Dried red chillies (*sookhi lal mirch*)

METHOD

1   Sort out the green leaves and cut the stems out.
    Shred the peeled balls into fine slices. Wash the
    leaves and knol khol slices together in a large
    vessel.

2   Heat the oil in a pressure cooker; add salt and
    asafoetida. Add sliced knol khol and leaves.
    Pour 1 cup water, stirring well with a ladle.
    Pressure cook on high heat for 15 minutes or
    till 3 whistles. Remove the lid of cooker under
    running tap water immediately.

3   Put the cooker on high heat again and cook the
    knol khol till the water dries up. Pour 3 cups
    water and dried red chillies. Bring to the boil for
    5 minutes.

4   Serve with steamed rice.

Dum Munj

FRIED KNOL KHOL IN YOGHURT

Serves: 6

INGREDIENTS

1 kg / 2.2 lb Knol khol (*kholrabi*), peeled,
    washed, cut into 2 cm-thick round pieces
1 cup / 220 ml / 7 fl oz Mustard oil for frying
½ tsp Asafoetida (*hing*)
2 Cloves (*laung*)
Salt to taste
3 tsp / 6 gm Red chilli powder
2 tbsp / 30 gm / 1 oz Yoghurt (*dahi*), whisked
1 tsp / 3 gm Ginger powder (*sonth*)
2 tsp / 6 gm Fennel (*saunf*) powder
1 tsp / 3 gm *Ver* masala (see p. 16)

METHOD

1   Heat the oil in a pan; fry the knol khol till
    golden brown.

2   In a separate vessel, take 3 tbsp oil from the
    pan. Add asafoetida, cloves, salt, 3 cups water,
    red chilli powder, yoghurt, ginger powder, and
    fennel powder; bring to the boil. Add fried
    knol kohl and mix well.

3   Cook for 10 minutes. Add *ver* masala and cook till
    the knol khol is tender and the gravy is thick.

4   Serve hot with steamed rice.

Dum Oluv
WHOLE SPICY POTATOES

Serves: 6

INGREDIENTS

1 kg / 2.2 lb Potatoes, round, medium-sized
2 cups / 440 ml / 15 fl oz Mustard / Refined oil
  for frying
2 Bay leaves (*tej patta*)
2 Cloves (*laung*)
1 tsp / 2 gm Cumin (*jeera*) seeds
1 Cinnamon (*dalchini*) stick
3 tsp / 6 gm Red chilli powder
Salt to taste
½ cup / 110 gm / 3½ oz Yoghurt (*dahi*)
1 tsp / 3 gm Ginger powder (*sonth*)
2 tsp / 6 gm Fennel (*saunf*) powder
1 tsp / 3 gm Black cardamom (*badi elaichi*)
  powder
1 tsp / 2½ gm Black cumin (*shah jeera*) seeds

METHOD

1 Boil the potatoes till tender. Peel the skin and prick the potatoes deep with a tooth pick or a fork.

2 Heat the oil in a deep pan; deep-fry the potatoes till golden brown.

3 Take the leftover oil in a separate vessel; add bay leaves, cloves, cumin seeds, cinnamon stick, red chilli powder, and salt. Add ½ cup water. Keep stirring till the mixture turns red. Whisk the yoghurt in a bowl and add to the gravy. Add 4 cups water, ginger powder, fennel powder, and cumin powder; mix well.

4 Add the fried potatoes to the gravy and boil on medium heat for 15 minutes. Simmer for another 15 minutes.

5 Add black cardamom powder and black cumin seeds; mix well. Serve with steamed rice or *nan*.

*Autumn in the Mughal Gardens,
Srinagar.
Photograph: Mukhtar Ahmad*

Haak

LEAFY GREENS

Serves: 6

INGREDIENTS

1 kg / 2.2 lb Kashmiri Spinach (*haak*)
1 cup / 220 ml / 7 fl oz Mustard oil
½ tsp Asafoetida (*hing*)
Salt to taste
5 Dried red chillies (*sookhi lal mirch*)

METHOD

1 Wash the green leaves and drain in a holed basket.

2 Heat the oil in a pressure cooker; add asafoetida and salt. Pour 6 cups water and bring to the boil. Add the leaves and keep stirring for a few minutes. Pressure cook for 10 minutes. Remove the lid under running tap water to retain the green colour.

3 Add dried red chillies and cook for 2 minutes.

4 Serve hot with steamed rice.

Note: Haak *is the main green leafy vegetable in a Kashmiri meal. If* haak *is not available cook leafy spinach the same way.*

Haak t, Nadir

GREENS WITH LOTUS STEMS

Serves: 6

INGREDIENTS

1 kg / 2.2 lb Kashmiri Spinach (*haak*), sort, stems chopped, washed
250 gm / 9 oz Lotus stems (*kamal kakri*), scraped, cut crosswise 2″ long
1 cup / 220 ml / 7 fl oz Mustard oil
Salt to taste
½ tsp Asafoetida (*hing*)
5 Dried red chillies (*sookhi lal mirch*)

METHOD

1 Heat the oil in a pressure cooker; add salt, asafoetida, and lotus stems. Fry for 5 minutes. Add 6 cups water and bring to the boil. Add greens and stir well. Pressure cook for 10 minutes.

2 Remove the lid under running water tap. Add dried red chillies and bring to the boil for 2 minutes.

3 Serve hot with steamed rice and yoghurt.

Note: This vegetarian dish is best served as an accompaniment to Rogan josh.

Moung Dal t, Nadir

GREEN GRAM LENTIL WITH LOTUS STEMS

Serves: 6

INGREDIENTS

500 gm / 1.1 lb Green gram whole (*moong*),
 soaked in warm water for 1 hour
250 gm / 9 oz Lotus stems (*kamal kakri*), washed,
 cut into 3 cm-long pieces
Salt to taste
1½ tsp / 4½ gm Turmeric (*haldi*) powder
1 tbsp / 15 ml Mustard oil
½ tsp Asafoetida (*hing*)
3 tsp / 9 gm Fennel (*saunf*) powder
1½ tsp / 4½ gm Ginger powder (*sonth*)
5 Dried red or green chillies

METHOD

1 Pressure cook the lentil and lotus stems with
 salt, turmeric powder and 4 cups water for
 10 minutes.

2 Heat the oil in a separate pan; add asafoetida,
 fennel powder, and ginger powder; stir. Add
 this to the lentil mixture in the pressure
 cooker and simmer for 5 minutes.

3 Serve hot garnished with dried red or
 green chillies.

Gogje t, Nadir

TURNIPS WITH LOTUS STEMS

Serves: 6

INGREDIENTS

1 kg / 2.2 lb Turnips (*shalgam*), peeled, cut
 crosswise, washed, drained
500 gm / 1.1 lb Lotus stems (*kamal kakri*),
 cleaned, cut crosswise, washed, drained
2 tbsp / 30 ml / 1 fl oz Mustard / Refined oil
Salt to taste
½ tsp Asafoetida (*hing*)
4 Dried red or green chillies
½ tsp *Ver* masala (see p. 16)

METHOD

1 Heat the oil in a pressure cooker; add salt,
 asafoetida, turnips, and lotus stems. Fry till the
 water dries up. Add 4 cups water and pressure
 cook for 5 minutes.

2 Remove the lid under running tap water and
 add dried red or green chillies. Bring to the boil
 till the gravy thickens. Sprinkle *ver* masala and
 serve hot.

3 This unique combination of vegetables can be
 enjoyed with steamed rice.

Razma t, Gogje

KIDNEY BEANS WITH TURNIPS

Serves: 6

INGREDIENTS

1 kg / 2.2 lb Kidney beans (*rajma*), soaked
  overnight, drained
1 kg / 2.2 lb Turnip (*shalgam*), peeled, cut into
  4-6 pieces
Salt to taste
2 tsp / 6 gm Ginger powder (*sonth*)
3 tsp / 9 gm Red chilli powder
½ tsp Asafoetida (*hing*)
2 tbsp / 30 ml / 1 fl oz Mustard / Refined oil
2 tsp / 6 gm *Ver* masala (see p. 16)

METHOD

1 Put the soaked beans in a pressure cooker. Add
  12 cups water, salt, 2 tsp ginger powder, red
  chilli powder, and asafoetida. Pressure cook for
  5 minutes or till one whistle. Remove the lid of
  the cooker and keep aside.

2 Heat the oil in a frying pan; fry the turnips for
  5 minutes.

3 Add the turnips to the kidney beans in the
  pressure cooker and cook with out pressure
  till the turnip gets cooked. Add *ver* masala and
  bring to the boil.

4 Serve with steamed rice.

*Note: This dish always tastes better if cooked the
previous day.*

Palak t, Nadir

MASHED SPINACH WITH LOTUS STEMS

Serves: 6

INGREDIENTS

1 kg / 2.2 lb Spinach (*palak*), discard stems,
  leaves washed
1 Lotus stem (*kamal kakri*), medium-sized,
  cleaned, cut into round 1 cm-thick pieces
½ cup / 110 ml / 3½ fl oz Mustard / Refined oil
½ tsp Asafoetida (*hing*)
Salt to taste
500 gm / 1.1 lb Tomatoes, chopped
2 tsp / 1½ gm Red chilli powder
1 tsp / 3 gm Ginger powder (*sonth*)
1 tsp / 3 gm *Ver* masala (see p. 16)

METHOD

1 Boil the spinach; keep stirring occasionally till
  tender. Drain the water in a strainer and keep
  the spinach aside. When cool, mash the spinach
  with clean hands.

2 Heat the oil in a vessel; fry the lotus stem till
  golden brown. Remove and keep aside. Add
  asafoetida, salt, and tomatoes; stir with a ladle
  to a smooth paste.

3 Add the mashed spinach, red chilli powder,
  and ginger powder; keep stirring till it is
  mixed well. Add ½ cup water and fried lotus
  stem; cook till the
  water dries up.
  Add *ver* masala
  and mix well.

4 Serve
  hot with
  steamed
  rice or
  chapatti.

Razma Hemb t Nadir

SPICY FRENCH BEANS WITH LOTUS STEMS

Serves: 6

INGREDIENTS

1 kg / 2.2 lb French beans, washed, cut into
  2″ pieces
250 gm / 9 oz Lotus stems (*kamal kakri*), peeled,
  cut into 1 cm-thick round slices
2 tbsp / 30 ml / 1 fl oz Refined oil
1 tsp / 2 gm Cumin (*jeera*) seeds
Salt to taste
2 tsp / 6 gm Red chilli powder
1 tsp / 3 gm Ginger powder (*sonth*)
3-4 Dried red chillies (*sookhi lal mirch*)

METHOD

1 Heat the oil in a frying pan; add French beans,
   lotus stems, cumin seeds, and salt. Cook on
   high heat for 10 minutes. Add red chilli powder
   and ginger powder; mix well. Simmer till the
   beans are tender.

2 Add dried red chillies and serve hot with
   chapatti, steamed rice or any dish of your choice.

Souchal t, Nadir

GREENS WITH FRIED LOTUS STEMS

Serves: 6

INGREDIENTS

1 kg / 2.2 lb Kashmiri *souchal*, sort out the leaves,
  discard the hard stems
250 gm / 9 oz Lotus stems (*kamal kakri*), washed,
  drained, cut into 1 cm-thick pieces
½ cup / 110 ml / 3½ fl oz Mustard oil
Salt to taste
½ tsp Asafoetida (*hing*)
2 tsp / 6 gm Red chilli powder
1 tsp / 3 gm *Ver* masala (see p. 16)
4 Dried red chillies (*sookhi lal mirch*)

METHOD

1 Fry the lotus stems in hot oil till golden brown.
   Remove and keep aside.

2 Take some oil in a pan; add salt, asafoetida, and
   souchal. Keep stirring on high heat till the water
   is absorbed. Add the fried lotus stems and mix
   well with a ladle.

3 Add red chilli powder and keep stirring till it
   dries. Sprinkle *ver* masala and mix well.

4 Serve garnished with dried red chillies and
   accompanied with steamed rice or *nan* or roti.

A gathering of women in their traditional outfits in the early 1900's.

Tamatar t, Nadir
LOTUS STEMS COOKED WITH TOMATOES

Serves: 6

INGREDIENTS

1 kg / 2.2 lb Lotus stems (*kamal kakri*), scraped,
   cut into 2″-long pieces, washed thoroughly
700 gm / 25 oz Tomatoes, chopped
½ cup / 110 ml / 3½ fl oz Mustard / Refined oil
Salt to taste
3 tsp / 9 gm Red chilli powder
2 tsp / 6 gm Ginger powder (*sonth*)
1 tsp / 3 gm Cumin (*jeera*) powder
2 tsp / 6 gm Fennel (*saunf*) powder (not used)

METHOD

1 Heat the mustard oil in a pressure cooker till
   smoking; fry the lotus stems for 5-10 minutes.
   Add tomatoes and stir with a ladle. Add salt and
   cook till the mixture becomes dry.

2 Add red chilli powder, ginger powder, cumin
   powder, and 3 cups water. Pressure cook for
   5 minutes. Remove the lid and simmer for
   5 minutes.

3 Serve hot with steamed rice, nan or chapatti.

Top: Navigating in the backwaters during winter.
Below: Heavy burden! Carrying hay long ago.

Tchok Nadir

LOTUS STEMS IN SOUR GRAVY

Serves: 6

INGREDIENTS

1 kg / 2.2 lb Lotus stems (*kamal kakri*), scraped, cut into 2″-long pieces, washed thoroughly
½ cup / 110 ml / 3½ fl oz Mustard / Refined oil
½ tsp Asafoetida (*hing*)
Salt to taste
1 tsp / 2 gm Cumin (*jeera*) seeds
3 tsp / 9 gm Red chilli powder
2 tsp / 6 gm Ginger powder (*sonth*)
3 tsp / 9 gm Fennel (*saunf*) powder
½ cup / 100 ml / 3½ fl oz Tamarind liquid

METHOD

1 Heat the oil in a pressure cooker; add asafoetida, salt, cumin seeds, and lotus stems. Fry for 10 minutes.

2 Add red chilli powder, ginger powder, fennel powder, and 3 cups water; stir and pressure cook for 5 minutes. Remove the lid and add tamarind liquid; cook till the gravy thickens.

3 Serve hot accompanied with any kind of dal or greens *(haak)*.

Vost Haak t, Nadir

RED COLOURED GREENS WITH LOTUS STEMS

Serves: 6

INGREDIENTS

1 kg / 2.2 lb Red greens (*vost haak*), leaves sorted, drained
200 gm / 7 oz Lotus stems (*kamal kakri*), washed, cut into small round pieces
½ cup / 110 ml / 3½ oz Mustard oil
½ tsp Asafoetida (*hing*)
Salt to taste
3 tsp / 9 gm Red chilli powder
2 tsp / 6 gm Ginger powder (*sonth*)
½ cup / 110 gm / 3½ oz Yoghurt (*dahi*), whisked
1 tsp / 3 gm *Ver* masala (see p. 16)

METHOD

1 Heat the oil in a pressure cooker; add asafoetida, salt, and *vost haak*. Mix well with a ladle and pressure cook for 10 minutes. Open the lid and cook on high heat.

2 Stir-fry the lotus stems in another pan. Remove and add to the cooker along with red chilli powder, ginger powder, and yoghurt; mix well till the gravy turns thick.

3 Add *ver* masala, mix well and simmer for 5 minutes.

4 Serve with steamed rice or anything of your choice.

Nadir Yakhni

LOTUS STEMS IN YOGHURT

Serves: 6

INGREDIENTS

1 kg / 2.2 lb Lotus stems (*kamal kakri*), scraped, washed, cut into 1″-long pieces
3 cups / 675 gm / 24 oz Yoghurt (*dahi*), whisked
½ cup / 110 ml / 3½ fl oz Mustard / Refined oil
2 Bay leaves (*tej patta*)
2 Cinnamon (*dalchini*) sticks
2 Cloves (*laung*)
3 tsp / 9 gm Fennel (*saunf*) powder
2 tsp / 6 gm Ginger powder (*sonth*)
Salt to taste
3 tsp / 9 gm Black cumin (*shah jeera*) seeds
3 Black cardamoms (*badi elaichi*), crushed
4 Green cardamoms (*choti elaichi*), crushed
1 tsp / 5 gm Cornflour

METHOD

1 Heat the oil in a pressure cooker; add bay leaves, cinnamon sticks, cloves, 6 cups water, fennel powder, ginger powder, and salt. Mix well.

2 Add lotus stems and pressure cook for 5 minutes. Remove the lid of the cooker and boil on high heat for 10 minutes or till the lotus stems are tender.

3 Add whisked yoghurt and black cumin seeds; mix well with a ladle and keep stirring. Add crushed black and green cardamom.

4 Mix the cornflour with 2 tsp water and pour into pressure cooker. Boil for 2 minutes and simmer for 2 minutes.

5 Serve with steamed rice and *dum oluv* (see p. 71).

A quick smoke in autumn.
Photograph: Mukhtar Ahmad

80

Wangen Yakhni

FRIED AUBERGINE IN YOGHURT

Serves: 6

INGREDIENTS

1 kg / 2.2 lb Aubergine (*baigan*), washed, cut into 4 pieces
2 cups / 450 gm / 1 lb Yoghurt (*dahi*), whisked
2 cups / 440 ml / 15 fl oz Refined oil for frying
Salt to taste
1 Bay leaf (*tej patta*)
2 tsp / 4 gm Cumin (*jeera*) seeds
1 Cinnamon (*dalchini*) stick
3 Cloves (*laung*)
3 tsp / 9 gm Fennel (*saunf*) powder
2 tsp / 6 gm Ginger powder (*sonth*)
1 tsp / 3 gm Cumin (*jeera*) powder
1 tsp / 2½ gm Black cumin (*shah jeera*) seeds
2 Green cardamoms (*choti elaichi*), coarsely ground
5 Green chillies, large ones

METHOD

1 Heat the oil in a frying pan; fry the aubergine till golden brown.

2 Take 1 tbsp oil in a separate pot; add salt, bay leaf, cumin seeds, cinnamon stick, cloves, and 4 cups water. Add fennel powder, ginger powder, and cumin powder; bring to the boil. Add yoghurt and keep stirring till it is mixed well with the gravy.

3 Add fried aubergine and cook for 5 minutes. Sprinkle black cumin seeds and green cardamom powder; mix well.

4 Serve hot garnished with green chillies and accompanied with steamed rice or chapatti or *nan*.

Note: While serving make sure the aubergines don't break.

Razma Hemb t, Wangen

FRENCH BEANS WITH AUBERGINE

Serves: 6

INGREDIENTS

1 kg / 2.2 lb French beans, washed, stringed, cut
into 2″ pieces

250 gm / 9 oz Aubergine (*baigan*), small ones,
washed, cut into 4 pieces

½ cup / 110 ml / 3½ fl oz Refined / Mustard oil
for frying

2 tbsp / 30 ml / 1 fl oz Oil for cooking

1 tsp / 2 gm Cumin (*jeera*) seeds

Salt to taste

2 tsp / 6 gm Red chilli powder

1 tsp / 3 gm Ginger powder (*sonth*)

1 tsp / 3 gm *Ver* masala (see p. 16)

4 Dried red chillies (*sookhi lal mirch*)

METHOD

1 Heat the oil in a frying pan; fry the aubergine
and keep aside.

2 Take 2 tbsp oil in a separate pan; add French
beans, cumin seeds, and salt; stir well and cook
for 10 minutes on high heat. Add red chilli
powder and ginger powder; stir and simmer for
10 minutes.

3 Add *ver* masala, dried red chillies, and fried
aubergine; stir once and serve hot with *nan*.

Tchont t, Wangen

COOKING APPLES WITH AUBERGINE

Serves: 6

INGREDIENTS

500 gm / 1.1 lb Cooking apples, washed, cut
into 4 pieces, deseeded, do not peel

250 gm / 9 oz Aubergine, (*baigan*), long ones,
washed, cut into 4 pieces

½ cup / 110 ml / 3½ fl oz Mustard / Refined oil
for frying

1 tbsp / 15 ml Oil for cooking

Salt to taste

1 tsp / 3 gm Red chilli powder

½ tsp / 1½ gm Ginger powder (*sonth*)

½ tsp / 1½ gm Turmeric (*haldi*) powder

3 Green chillies

METHOD

1 Heat the oil in a pan; fry the aubergine till
crispy brown. Remove and keep aside.

2 Fry the apples in the same oil, turning once.
Remove them carefully so that they do not
break.

3 Take 1 tbsp oil in a separate pan; add salt, red
chilli powder, ginger powder, turmeric powder,
and 2 cups water. Bring to the boil. Add fried
apples and aubergine and cook for 2 minutes
on high heat. Add green chillies and serve hot
with steamed rice.

Souchal t, Wangen

KASHMIRI SPINACH WITH AUBERGINE

Serves: 6

INGREDIENTS

1 kg / 2.2 lb Kashmiri Spinach (*haak*), discard the
  hard stems, washed, drained
250 gm / 9 oz Aubergine (*baigan*), small, cut into
  4 pieces, washed, drained
½ cup / 110 ml / 3½ fl oz Mustard oil
½ tsp Asafoetida (*hing*)
Salt to taste
2 tsp / 6 gm Red chilli powder
4 Dried red chillies (*sookhi lal mirch*)
1 tsp / 3 gm *Ver* masala (see p. 16)

METHOD

1 Heat the oil in a pan; fry the aubergine till
  brown. Keep aside.

2 In the same oil, add asafoetida, salt, and
  Kashmiri spinach; stirring till the leaves are a
  little tender.

3 Add red chilli powder and mix well. Add fried
  aubergine and dried red chillies; mix. Sprinkle
  ver masala mix and serve hot.

Tamater t, Wangen

TOMATOES WITH AUBERGINE

Serves: 6

INGREDIENTS

1 kg / 2.2 lb Aubergine (*baigan*), long ones,
  washed, cut length wise into 2 pieces
700 gm / 25 oz Tomatoes, chopped
2 cups / 440 ml / 15 fl oz Refined oil for frying
3 tsp / 9 gm Red chilli powder
½ tsp / 1½ gm Cumin (*jeera*) seeds
2 tsp / 6 gm Ginger powder (*sonth*)
Salt to taste
5 Green chillies

METHOD

1 Heat the oil in a deep-frying pan; fry the
  aubergine till light brown. Keep aside.

2 Take 1 tbsp oil in a separate pot; add tomatoes
  and cook for 10 minutes. Add red chilli powder,
  cumin seeds, 4 cups water, ginger powder, and
  salt; bring to the boil.

3 Add fried aubergine and green chillies; cook on
  high heat for 5 minutes.

4 Serve hot with steamed rice or any thing of
  your choice.

'If there is heaven on Earth, it is here, it is here, it is here,' uttered Jehangir when he first set his eyes upon Kashmir in the seventeenth century. The beautiful Chinar (maple) trees and their leaves lend a touch of gold to the Mughal Gardens in Srinagar.
Photograph: Mukhtar Ahmad

85

Tchok Wangen

TANGY AUBERGINE

Serves: 6

INGREDIENTS

1 kg / 2.2 lb Aubergine (*baigan*), long ones, cut
   into 4 long pieces, washed, drained
2 cups / 440 ml / 15 fl oz Mustard oil for frying
2 Cloves (*laung*)
Salt to taste
3 tsp / 9 gm Red chilli powder
1 tsp / 3 gm Ginger powder (*sonth*)
2 tsp / 6 gm Fennel (*saunf*) powder
1 tsp / 3 gm *Ver* masala (see p. 16)
½ cup / 100 ml / 3½ fl oz Tamarind liquid
5 Green chillies

METHOD

1 Heat the oil in a deep-frying pan; fry the
  aubergine till golden brown. Take them out of
  the pan.

2 In a separate vessel, take 2 tbsp oil; add cloves,
  salt, red chilli powder, and 4 cups water. Add
  rest of the spices and tamarind liquid; bring to
  the boil.

3 Add fried aubergine and cook on high flame for
  5 minutes.

4 Serve hot garnished with green chillies and
  accompanied with steamed rice.

Al Rogan Josh

PUMPKIN IN RED GRAVY

Serves: 6

INGREDIENTS

1 kg / 2.2 lb Pumpkin (*kaddu*), peeled, cut into
  pieces 3 cm wide
2 cups / 440 ml / 15 fl oz Mustard / Refined oil
  for frying
½ tsp Asafoetida (*hing*)
2 Cloves (*laung*)
2 Black cardamom (*badi elaichi*), crushed
1 Cinnamon (*dalchini*) stick
Salt to taste
3 tsp / 9 gm Red chilli powder
2 tsp / 6 gm Ginger powder (*sonth*)
3 tsp / 9 gm Fennel (*saunf*) powder
1½ cups / 335 gm / 11½ oz Yoghurt (*dahi*),
  whisked well
1 tsp / 2½ gm Black cumin (*shah jeera*) seeds
3 Green cardamoms (*choti elaichi*), crushed

METHOD

1 Heat the oil in a deep pan; deep-fry the
  pumpkin till golden brown.

2 Take 3 tbsp oil in another vessel; add asafoetida,
  cloves, black cardamom, cinnamon stick, salt,
  red chilli powder, 2 cups water, ginger powder,
  and fennel powder. Bring to the boil. Add
  yoghurt and keep stirring. Add fried pumpkin
  and cook till the gravy thickens.

3 Sprinkle black cumin
  seeds and green
  cardamom powder
  and simmer
  for 2 minutes.
  Remove and
  serve hot.

Al Yakhni

BOTTLE GOURD IN YOGHURT

Serves: 6

INGREDIENTS

1 kg / 2.2 lb Bottle gourd (*lauki*), peeled, cut
    into 3 cm-long and 2 cm-wide pieces
2 cups / 450 gm / 1 lb Yoghurt (*dahi*), whisked
2 cups / 440 ml / 15 fl oz Mustard / Refined oil
    for frying
2 tbsp / 30 ml Oil for cooking
2 Cinnamon (*dalchini*) sticks
3 Cloves (*laung*)
2 Bay leaves (*tej patta*)
1 tsp / 2 gm Cumin (*jeera*) seeds
Salt to taste
3 tsp / 9 gm Fennel (*saunf*) powder
2 tsp / 6 gm Ginger powder (*sonth*)
2 Black cardamoms (*badi elaichi*), crushed
2 tsp / 5 gm Black cumin (*shah jeera*) seeds
3 Green cardamoms (*choti elaichi*), crushed

METHOD

1 Heat the oil in pan; deep-fry the bottle gourd
   in hot oil till golden brown.

2 Take 2 tbsp oil from the pan in a separate
   vessel; add cinnamon sticks, cloves, bay
   leaves, cumin seeds, salt, 3 cups water, fennel
   powder, and ginger powder. Bring to the boil.
   Add yoghurt and stir well with a ladle. Add
   fried bottle gourd and cook till the gravy
   thickens. Sprinkle black cumin seeds and
   green cardamom powder; mix well.

3 Serve with rice or chapatti.

*A villager smoking a hookah outside his house.
Photograph:
Mukhtar Ahmad*

Kanguch Yakhni

MORELS IN YOGHURT SAUCE

Serves: 6

INGREDIENTS

250 gm / 9 oz
   Mushrooms
   (*morels*), washed,
   cleaned, soaked in
   warm water for 30
   minutes
½ cup / 110 ml / 3½ oz Mustard oil
2 Cloves (*laung*)
½ tsp Asafoetida (*hing*)
1 Cinnamon (*dalchini*) stick
1 Bay leaf (*tej patta*)
Salt to taste
2 tsp / 6 gm Fennel (*saunf*) powder
1 tsp / 3 gm Ginger powder (*sonth*)
1 tsp / 3 gm Cumin (*jeera*) powder
500 gm / 1.1 lb Yoghurt (*dahi*), whisked
2 Black cardamoms (*badi elaichi*), crushed
4 Green cardamoms (*choti elaichi*), crushed
1 tsp / 2½ gm Black cumin (*shah jeera*) seeds

METHOD

1 Heat the oil in a pot; add cloves, asafoetida
   cinnamon stick, bay leaf, salt, and mushrooms.
   Fry for a few minutes. Pour 2 cups water and
   fennel powder, ginger powder, and cumin
   powder. Cook till the mushrooms are tender.

2 Add whisked yoghurt and keep stirring gently
   so that the mushrooms do not break.

3 Add black and green cardamoms and black
   cumin seeds. Simmer for 5 minutes or till the
   gravy thickens.

4 Serve with steamed rice, chapatti or *nan*.

*Note: This is a special kind of wild mushroom found
in the hills of Kashmir.*

Phool Rogan Josh

CAULIFLOWER IN THICK RED GRAVY

Serves: 6

INGREDIENTS

1 kg / 2.2 lb Cauliflower (*phool gobi*), cut into
   single florets
2 cups / 440 ml / 15 fl oz Mustard / Refined oil
   for frying
3 tbsp / 45 ml / 1½ fl oz Oil for cooking
½ tsp Asafoetida (*hing*)
2 Cloves (*laung*)
1 Cinnamon (*dalchini*) stick
1 Bay leaf (*tej patta*)
Salt to taste
3 tsp / 6 gm Red chilli powder
½ cup / 110 gm / 3½ oz Yoghurt (*dahi*), whisked
2 tsp / 6 gm Fennel (*saunf*) powder
1 tsp / 3 gm Ginger powder (*sonth*)
1 tsp / 2 gm Cumin (*jeera*) seeds
1 tsp / 3 gm Black cardamom (*badi elaichi*)
powder

METHOD

1 Heat the oil in a pan; fry the cauliflower till
   crispy brown.

2 Heat 3 tbsp oil in a pot; add asafoetida, cloves,
   cinnamon stick, bay leaf, salt, red chilli powder,
   and yoghurt. Stir well. Add 2 cups water,
   fennel powder, ginger powder, and cumin
   seeds; boil on high heat. Add fried cauliflower
   and cook till the gravy turns
   thick. Sprinkle black
   cardamom powder.

3 Serve with
   steamed rice,
   chapatti
   or *nan*.

Kanguch t, Chaman

MORELS AND COTTAGE CHEESE IN YOGHURT

Serves: 6

INGREDIENTS

250 gm / 9 oz Mushrooms (*morels*), soaked in
   warm water for 30 minutes
500 gm / 1.1 lb Cottage cheese (*paneer*), cut into
   medium-sized pieces
1 cup / 220 ml / 7 fl oz Mustard / Refined oil
2 Cloves (*laung*)
½ tsp Asafoetida (*hing*)
1 tsp / 2 gm Cumin (*jeera*) seeds
1 tsp / 3 gm Turmeric (*haldi*) powder
3 tsp / 9 gm Fennel (*saunf*) powder
2 tsp / 6 gm Ginger powder (*sonth*)
1 tsp / 3 gm Cumin powder
Salt to taste
2 tsp / 6 gm Fenugreek (*methi*) powder
½ cup / 110 gm / 3½ oz Yoghurt (*dahi*), whisked

METHOD

1 Fry the cottage cheese in hot oil till light brown.
   Keep aside.

2 Take 3 tbsp oil from the same pan; add cloves,
   asafoetida, cumin seeds and mushrooms. Cook
   for 5 minutes. Add 4 cups water and all the
   powdered spices; bring to the boil. Add fried
   cottage cheese and cook on medium heat till
   the gravy thickens.

3 Add whisked yoghurt just before serving.

4 Serve with steamed rice, *nan* or chapatti.

Chaman t Meeth

COTTAGE CHEESE IN FENUGREEK SAUCE

Serves: 6

INGREDIENTS

500 gm / 1.1 lb Cottage cheese (*paneer*), sliced
   into 1″-thick square pieces
250 gm / 9 oz Fenugreek (*methi*), cleaned,
   washed
½ cup / 110 ml / 3½ fl oz Mustard / Refined oil
¹/₃ tsp Asafoetida (*hing*)
Salt to taste
2 tsp / 6 gm Red chilli powder
1 tsp / 3 gm Ginger powder (*sonth*)
1 tsp / 3 gm Turmeric (*haldi*) powder
2 Cloves (*laung*)

METHOD

1 Boil fenugreek in a large vessel for 10 minutes.
   Drain the water and keep aside to cool. Mash
   with hands or grind in a mixer.

2 Heat the oil in a pan; fry the cottage cheese and
   keep aside.

3 In the same oil, add asafoetida, salt and
   fenugreek and fry for 2 minutes. Add red chilli
   powder and all other spices.

4 Add 3 cups water and bring to the boil. Add
   fried cottage cheese (optional, you can just add
   cottage cheese without frying) and cook for
   10 minutes till the gravy thickens.

5 Serve with the main course.

Chaman Kaliya

COTTAGE CHEESE IN YELLOW GRAVY

Serves: 6

INGREDIENTS

1 kg / 2.2 lb Cottage cheese (*paneer*), sliced into
  1″ -thick and 2″-long pieces
1 cup / 220 ml / 7 fl oz Mustard / Refined oil
  for frying
3 Cloves (*laung*)
½ tsp Asafoetida (*hing*)
2 Bay leaves (*tej patta*)
1 tsp / 2 gm Cumin (*jeera*) seeds
2 tsp / 6 gm Turmeric (*haldi*) powder
3 tsp / 9 gm Fennel (*saunf*) powder
2 tsp / 6 gm Ginger powder (*sonth*)
1 tsp / 3 gm Cumin powder
Salt to taste
½ cup / 120 ml / 4 fl oz Milk
3 Black cardamoms (*badi elaichi*), crushed
3 Green cardamoms (*choti elaichi*), crushed
3 tsp / 9 gm Fenugreek (*methi*) powder

METHOD

1 Heat the oil in a non-stick frying pan; fry the cottage cheese slices till light brown tuning each side. Leave aside.

2 Take 3 tbsp oil in a deep vessel; add cloves, asafoctida, bay leaves, and cumin seeds; keep stirring for a second. Add 6 cups water, turmeric powder, fennel powder, ginger powder, cumin powder, and salt to taste; bring to the boil.

3 Add fried cottage cheese and cook on high hcat till the gravy thickens and cheese is soft. Add hot milk to the mixture and boil for 2 minutes till the milk merges with the gravy.

4 Add crushed black and green cardamoms and fenugreek powder; mix well.

5 Serve hot with steamed rice or chapatti.

Facing page: Kashmir's Mona Lisa amidst the lush mustard fields.
Photograph: Mukhtar Ahmad

Wangen Hetch, Tamber Lagith

DRIED AUBERGINE IN TAMARIND SAUCE

Serves: 6

INGREDIENTS

250 gm / 9 oz Dried Aubergine (*baigan*), washed
½ cup / 100 ml / 3½ fl oz Tamarind (*imli*) liquid
½ cup / 110 ml / 3½ fl oz Mustard oil
Salt to taste
½ tsp Asafoetida (*hing*)
2 tsp / 6 gm Red chilli powder
1 tsp / 2 gm Cumin (*jeera*) seeds
1 tsp / 3 gm Ginger powder (*sonth*)
1 tsp / 3 gm Fennel (*saunf*) powder
1 tsp / 3 gm *Ver* masala (see p. 16)

METHOD

1 Boil the aubergine in a pot with 8 cups water till half tender. Remove and squeeze gently. Keep aside and make sure they do not break.

2 Heat the oil in a separate vessel; add salt, asafoetida, and aubergine; fry till light brown. Add red chilli powder, cumin seeds, 4 cups water, ginger powder, and fennel powder; cook for 2 minutes on high heat. Add tamarind liquid and boil for a minute. Add *ver* masala; mix well.

3 Serve hot with steamed rice.

Al Hetch in Zamudud

DRIED BOTTLE GOURD IN YOGHURT

Serves: 6

INGREDIENTS

250 gm / 9 oz Dried bottle gourd (*lauki*), washed
4 tbsp / 60 ml / 2 fl oz Mustard oil
Salt to taste
½ tsp Asafoetida (*hing*)
1 Bay leaf (*tej patta*)
2 Cloves (*laung*)
1 tsp / 3 gm Ginger powder (*sonth*)
2 tsp / 6 gm Fennel (*saunf*) powder
1 tsp / 2 gm Cumin (*jeera*) seeds
2 cups / 450 gm / 1 lb Yoghurt (*dahi*), whisked
1 tsp / 2½ gm Black cumin (*shah jeera*) seeds
2 Green cardamoms (*choti elaichi*), crushed

METHOD

1 Boil the bottle gourd in a pot with 8 cups water till half tender. Remove and squeeze gently. Keep aside.

2 Heat the oil in a pot; add salt, asafoetida, bay leaf, cloves, and bottle gourd. Cook for 2 minutes. Add 2 cups water, ginger powder, fennel powder, and cumin seeds. Boil on high heat till the gravy thickens.

3 Add whisked yoghurt and stir well. Add black cumin seeds and crushed green cardamom.

4 Serve hot with steamed rice.

Haak t, Chaman

KASHMIRI SPINACH WITH COTTAGE CHEESE

Serves: 6

INGREDIENTS

1 kg / 2.2 lb Kashmiri Spinach (*haak*), cleaned, washed
500 gm / 1.1 lb Cottage cheese (*paneer*), sliced into 2″-long x ½″-thick, square pieces
1 cup / 220 ml / 7 fl oz Mustard oil
½ tsp Asafoetida (*hing*)
Salt to taste
2 Cloves (*laung*)
2 tsp / 6 gm Turmeric (*haldi*) powder
2 tsp / 6 gm Ginger powder (*sonth*)
3 tsp / 9 gm Fennel (*saunf*) powder
5 Green chillies

METHOD

1 Heat the oil in a deep pan; fry the cottage cheese till light brown. Keep aside.

2 Take same leftover oil in a pressure cooker; add asafoetida, salt, cloves, 8 cups water, turmeric powder, ginger powder, and fennel powder. Bring to the boil on high heat.

3 Add Kashmiri spinach and pressure cook for 5 minutes. Remove the lid, add fried cottage cheese and cook till the cheese becomes soft.

4 Serve hot garnished with green chillies.

Thool Razma Yakhni

GREEN KIDNEY BEANS IN YOGHURT

Serves: 6

INGREDIENTS

1 kg / 2.2 lb Green beans, shelled
¼ cup / 55 ml / 1¾ fl oz Refined / Mustard oil
Salt to taste
½ tsp Asafoetida (*hing*)
2 Cloves (*laung*)
1 Bay leaf (*tej patta*)
3 tsp / 9 gm Fennel (*saunf*) powder
2 tsp / 6 gm Ginger powder (*sonth*)
2 cups / 450 gm / 1 lb Yoghurt (*dahi*), whisked
2 Black cardamoms (*badi elaichi*), crushed
3 Green cardamoms (*choti elaichi*), crushed
½ tsp / 1¼ gm Black cumin (*shah jeera*) seeds
½ tsp Asafoetida

METHOD

1 Heat the oil in a pressure cooker; add asafoetida, the green beans, salt, cloves, and bay leaf. Fry for 5 minutes. Add 3 cups water, fennel powder, and ginger powder. Pressure cook for 2 minutes.

2 Add whisked yoghurt and mix well. Add crushed black and green cardamoms and black cumin seeds; mix well. Serve hot.

Karel t, Wangen Dued Lagith

BITTER GOURD AND AUBERGINE IN YOGHURT

Serves: 6

INGREDIENTS

500 gm / 1.1 lb Bitter gourd (*karela*), scraped, cut
  lengthwise, deseeded
250 gm / 9 oz Aubergine (*baigan*), small, washed,
  cut into 2 pieces
1 cup / 225 gm / 8 oz Yoghurt (*dahi*), whisked
½ cup / 110 ml / 3½ fl oz Mustard / Refined oil
2 Cloves (*laung*)
¼ tsp Asafoetida (*hing*)
1 tsp / 3 gm Ginger powder (*sonth*)
2 tsp / 6 gm Fennel (*saunf*) powder
Salt to taste
1 tsp / 3 gm Cumin (*jeera*) powder
1 tsp / 2 gm Cumin seeds
3 Green chillies

METHOD

1 Sprinkle salt all over the bitter gourd and keep
aside for an hour. Wash and squeeze water from
the bitter gourd with your palm.

2 Heat the oil in a frying pan; fry the aubergine
till light brown. Remove and fry the bitter
gourd in the same oil.

3 Take the leftover oil in a separate pot; add
cloves, asafoetida, 2 cups water, all the
powered spices, and cumin seeds. Bring to the
boil. Add yoghurt, stirring and mixing well
with the gravy.

4 Add fried bottle gourd and aubergine; cook for
5 minutes or till the gravy thickens.

5 Serve hot garnished with green chillies and
accompanied with steamed rice or chapatti.

Gurdol t, Oluv

RAW PLUM WITH POTATOES

Serves: 6

INGREDIENTS

500 gm / 1.1 lb Raw plums (*gurdol*), washed
1 kg / 2.2 lb Potatoes, peeled, washed, cut into
  6 pieces
3 tbsp / 45 ml / 1½ fl oz Mustard / Refined oil
2 tsp / 6 gm Red chilli powder
Salt to taste
2 tsp / 6 gm Ginger powder (*sonth*)
6 Green chillies

METHOD

1 Heat the oil in a deep pan; add the potatoes and
   fry for 10 minutes. Add red chilli powder, salt,
   4 cups water, and ginger powder; cook till the
   potatoes are tender.

2 Add the plums to the potato mixture and bring
   to the boil. Cook till the plums are tender.

3 Remove and garnish with green chillies. Serve
   with steamed rice.

Verifol t, Oluv

SUN-DRIED BLACK LENTILS WITH POTATOES

Serves: 6

INGREDIENTS

100 gm / 3½ oz Dried black gram dumplings
  (*vadi*), washed, drained quickly to avoid getting
  soggy
500 gm / 1.1 lb Potatoes, peeled, washed, cut
  into 6 pieces
3 tbsp / 45 ml / 1½ fl oz Mustard / Refined oil
2 tsp / 6 gm Red chilli powder
1 tsp / 3 gm Ginger powder (*sonth*)
Salt to taste
½ cup / 110 gm / 3½ oz Yoghurt (*dahi*), whisked

METHOD

1 Heat the oil in a deep pot; fry the dumplings for
   2 minutes. Remove to a plate.

2 Fry the potatoes in the same oil for
   5-10 minutes. Add red chilli powder, 4 cups
   water, ginger powder, and salt. Add fried
   dumplings and cook till tender.

3 Add whisked yoghurt and cook till the gravy
   thickens.

4 Serve with steamed rice or chapatti.

Al Kanej t, Wangen

PUMPKIN GREENS WITH AUBERGINE

Serves: 6

INGREDIENTS

1 kg / 2.2 lb Pumpkin greens, discard long
    rough stems, washed, drained
250 gm / 9 oz Aubergine (*baigan*), long ones, cut
    into 6 pieces, washed, drained
½ cup / 110 ml / 3½ fl oz Mustard oil
½ tsp Asafoetida (*hing*)
Salt to taste
3 tsp / 9 gm Red chilli powder
2 tsp / 6 gm Ginger powder (*sonth*)
2 tsp / 6 gm *Ver* masala (see p. 16)
5 Dried red chillies (*sookhi lal mirch*)

METHOD

1 Heat the oil in a pan; fry the aubergine till light
   brown. Remove.

2 In the same oil, add asafoetida, salt, and
   pumpkin greens; mix well with a ladle and fry
   till the water dries up and it is half tender.

3 Add red chilli powder, ginger powder, and *ver*
   masala; keep stirring. Add fried aubergine and
   dried red chillies. Cook for a minute.

4 Serve with steamed rice.

Note: This dish is a speciality of Kashmir cuisine.

Muj Pattar t, Wangen

RADISH LEAVES WITH AUBERGINE

Serves: 6

INGREDIENTS

1 kg / 2.2 lb Radish (*mooli*) with leaves, scraped,
    diced
250 gm / 9 oz Aubergine (*baigan*), long ones,
    washed, cut into 4 pieces
½ cup / 110 ml / 3½ fl oz Mustard oil for frying
2 tbsp / 30 ml / 1 fl oz Oil for cooking
½ tsp Asafoetida (*hing*)
5 Dried red chillies (*sookhi lal mirch*)
Salt to taste
1 tsp / 3 gm *Ver* masala (see p. 16)

METHOD

1 Clean the radish leaves separately by cutting the
   stems out. Wash well.

2 Put 8 cups water in a pressure cooker. Add
   radish and leaves together and pressure cook
   for 15 minutes or till 4 whistles. Remove the
   lid and wash the steamed radish and leaves
   under running tap water and squeeze gently.
   Keep aside.

3 Heat the oil in a frying pan; fry the aubergine
   till light brown.

4 Heat 2 tbsp oil in a vessel; add asafoetida, salt,
   and squeezed leaves and radish; fry for 5 minutes.
   Pour 6 cups water and bring to the boil. Add
   dried red chillies, salt, and fried aubergine; cook
   for 5 minutes and sprinkle *ver* masala.

5 Serve hot.

*Facing page: Sunset in the Dal Lake - truly overpowering
and awe inspiring!
Photographer: Wajid Drabu*

A typical village scene in autumn when chillies are left in the sun to dry.

RICE & BREAD

100 BATH
Steamed rice

100 MATTAR TAHER
Yellow rice

101 NENI PULAO
Lamb pulao

102 TAHER T, CHARVAN
Yellow rice with liver

102 MODUR PULAO
Sweet rice with dry fruits

103 KANGACH PULAO
Mushroom pulao

103 SHAKER PARE
Bread made of chestnut flour

105 CHER CHOT
Rice flour pancakes

105 ROTH
Sweet fried flour breads

Batha

STEAMED RICE

Serves: 6

INGREDIENTS

1 kg / 2.2 lb Basmati rice, washed
10 cups / 2.5 lt Water

METHOD

1 Mix rice and water in a large vessel and bring to the boil. When the rice is half cooked, drain all the water and continue to cook on low heat for 15 minutes.

2 Serve hot.

Note: By discarding the water the calorie content reduces. I will not suggest to absorb the water as done usually.

Mattar Taher

YELLOW RICE

Serves: 6

INGREDIENTS

3 cups / 600 gm / 22 oz Rice, washed
200 gm / 7 oz Green peas (*hara mattar*), peeled
½ tsp / 1½ gm Turmeric (*haldi*) powder
Salt to taste
2 tbsp / 30 ml / 1 fl oz Mustard oil, heated

METHOD

1 Boil the peas in a pot for 5 minutes and drain out the water.

2 Cook the rice in a vessel with 8 cups water. Add turmeric powder and mix well with a ladle. Bring to the boil, add peas and boil together till half tender; drain out the water.

3 Return to heat and cook on low heat for 15 minutes.

4 In a large plate transfer the yellow rice and mix with oil and salt.

5 Serve with pickles.

Note: Taher is cooked on birthdays and special occasions in Pandit homes.

Neni Pulao

LAMB PULAO

Serves: 6-8

INGREDIENTS

1 kg / 2.2 lb Basmati rice, washed, soaked, drained
700 gm / 25 oz Lamb
2 tsp / 6 gm Turmeric (*haldi*) powder
2 tsp / 6 gm Ginger powder (*sonth*)
Salt to taste
4 Cloves (*laung*)
2 Bay leaves (*tej patta*)
2 tsp / 4 gm Cumin (*jeera*) seeds
6 Green cardamoms (*choti elaichi*), crushed
6 Green chillies, cut into pieces
½ tsp Saffron (*kesar*)
3 Onions, chopped, fried brown
$^1/_3$ cup Ghee / Refined oil
4 Black cardamoms (*badi elaichi*), crushed

METHOD

1 Put the lamb in a pressure cooker with 6 cups water, turmeric powder, ginger powder, salt, cloves, bay leaves, and cumin seeds. Pressure cook for 10 minutes. Remove from heat and keep aside to cool.

2 Boil rice separately in 12 cups water. When half tender, drain the water out completely.

3 Open the lid of the cooker and in a separate large vessel mix the drained rice and lamb together. Add crushed green cardamom and green chillies in layers. Top with saffron, onions, and ghee/ refined oil. Sprinkle crushed black cardamom and cook on low heat for 30 minutes.

4 Serve with *kabargah* (see p. 43) and any kind of pickle.

The cool and calm grandeur of winter snow in Srinagar.

Taher t, Charvan
YELLOW RICE WITH LIVER

Serves: 6

INGREDIENTS

1 kg / 2.2 lb Rice
500 gm / 1.1 lb Liver, cut into cubes, washed, drained
3 tbsp / 45 ml / 1½ fl oz Mustard oil
Salt to taste
2 tsp / 6 gm Red chilli powder
2 tsp / 6 gm Turmeric (*haldi*) powder

METHOD

1 Heat 2 tbsp oil in a deep pot; add liver and fry till dark brown. Add salt, red chilli powder, 1 tsp turmeric powder and 2 cups water; cook till the liver is tender. Remove from heat.

2 Boil rice with 1 tsp turmeric powder separately. When rice is half cooked, drain out the water. Return to heat and cook on low heat for 15 minutes.

3 In a large pot, mix the rice and liver together and serve with *munj aanchar* (see p.114).

Modur Pulao
SWEET RICE WITH DRY FRUITS

Serves: 6

INGREDIENTS

1 kg / 2.2 lb Rice, washed
1 cup / 200 gm / 7 oz Sugar
4 Green cardamoms (*choti elaichi*), crushed
4 Black cardamoms (*badi elaichi*), crushed
2 tsp Saffron (*kesar*)
2 cups / 400 gm / 14 oz Ghee
½ cup / 70 gm / 2¼ oz Raisins (*kishmish*), soaked, washed
½ cup / 70 gm / 2¼ oz Almonds (*badam*), soaked, peeled
¼ cup / 20 gm Dry coconut (*nariyal*), pared, shredded
$^1/_3$ cup Dry dates (*khajur*), deseeded, cut length wise
4 Cloves (*laung*)
2 Bay leaves (*tej patta*)
2 Cinnamon (*dalchini*) sticks

METHOD

1 Boil the rice in 10 cups water. When half cooked, drain all the water out. Remove from heat.

2 Boil the sugar in 3 cups water to make syrup. Add green and black cardamoms. Add saffron and boil till the sugar dissolves completely.

3 Heat the ghee in a pan; add raisins, almonds, coconut, dates, cloves, bay leaves, and cinnamon sticks and sauté. Add half cooked rice and the syrup; mix well and cook on very low heat for 30 minutes.

4 Serve hot.

Kangach Pulao

MOREL PULAO

Serves: 6

INGREDIENTS

3 cups / 600 gm / 22 oz Basmati rice, soaked
   for 10 minutes
100 gm / 3½ fl oz Morels (*guchhi*), soaked for 10
   minutes,
6 tbsp / 90 ml / 3 fl oz Refined oil / Ghee
4 Cloves (*laung*)
5 Green cardamoms (*choti elaichi*)
5 Black cardamoms (*badi elaichi*)
2 Bay leaves (*tej patta*)
½ cup / 70 gm / 2¼ oz Almonds (*badam*),
   blanched
Salt to taste
2 tsp / 6 gm Ginger powder (*sonth*)
½ tsp / 1½ gm Turmeric (*haldi*) powder
1 tsp Saffron (*kesar*) extract

METHOD

1 Heat the ghee / oil in a heavy-bottomed pot;
add, cloves, green and black cardamoms, bay
leaves, and almonds; stir for 2 minutes. Add salt
and mushrooms; fry for 2-3 minutes.

2 Add soaked rice and stir well. Add 3 cups
water, ginger powder, turmeric powder, salt,
and saffron extract; mix well and simmer.
Cook, covered, till the rice and mushrooms are
cooked well.

3 Serve hot.

Shaker Pare

SWEET BREAD MADE OF CHESTNUT FLOUR

Serves: 6

INGREDIENTS

1 kg / 2.2 lb Chestnut flour (*sin gaada*)
2 cups / 400 gm / 14 oz Sugar
1¼ cups / 250 gm / 9 oz Ghee
3 cups / 660 ml / 21 fl oz Refined oil for frying

METHOD

1 Boil the sugar in a deep pot with 2 cups water
till the sugar dissolves completely. Remove
from heat and keep aside to cool.

2 Mix the ghee with the flour and knead with
warm sugar syrup.

3 Roll the dough out to make a thick chapatti.
Cut with a knife into square pieces (this is called
shaker pare).

4 Heat the oil in a pan; deep-fry the *shaker
pare* till brown. Remove and keep aside to
cool. Then store in an airtight jar and enjoy
whenever you wish.

*Note: This snack is made in Pandit festivals especially
on thread ceremony. This snack is meant for those
who are fasting. You can make salty* shaker pare *also
by using salt instead of sugar.*

The floating vegetable gardens on the Dal Lake.

Cher Chot

RICE FLOUR PANCAKES

Serves: 4

INGREDIENTS

1 cup / 100 gm / 3½ oz Rice flour
Salt to taste
½ tsp / 1¼ gm Black cumin (*shah jeera*) seeds
½ cup / 110 ml / 3½ fl oz Refined oil

METHOD

1 Mix the rice flour with 1 cup water and make a thick paste of dropping consistency.

2 Add salt and black cumin seeds and mix well.

3 Heat about 1 tsp oil in a non-stick frying pan; put ½ cup rice flour mixture in the pan and spread evenly. Fry both sides, turning upside down, till golden brown and crisp. Remove and repeat till all the batter is used up.

4 Serve with *kehwa* (see p. 120) or any other kind of tea.

Roth

SWEET FRIED FLOUR BREAD

Serves: 6

INGREDIENTS

1 kg / 2.2 lb Flour (*maida*)
1½ cups / 300 gm / 11 oz Sugar
1 cup / 200 gm / 7 oz Ghee for mixing
5 Black cardamoms (*badi elaichi*), coarsely ground
Refined oil / Ghee for deep-frying
½ cup Poppy seeds (*khus khus*)

METHOD

1 Heat 4 cups water, add sugar and boil till the sugar dissolves completely. Remove and keep aside to cool.

2 In a large bowl, add flour, ghee, black cardamom, and the sugar syrup. Knead well and make a hard dough.

3 Take some dough about 3-4″-thick and roll out into a circular chapatti. Make flowery designs with a toothpick or a fork / spoon.

4 Heat the oil / ghee in a pan; deep-fry the chapatti on slow heat till golden brown. Remove and quickly sprinkle poppy seeds on one side. Repeat till all are fried.

5 Serve with *sheer chai* (see p. 120).

Note: Roth is prepared in the Pandit festival of Pun which falls in the month of September. It is a must for everyone in the family to get a share. I always look forward to this festival to enjoy roth.

Scarlet chillies festoon the windows of village homes.
A unique way of drying chillies in Kashmir!
Photograph: Mukhtar Ahmad

CHUTNEYS & PICKLES

Anardan Chetin

POMEGRANATE CHUTNEY

Serves: 6

INGREDIENTS

1 cup Pomegranate (*anar dana*)
Salt to taste

METHOD

1 Wash pomegranate thoroughly.

2 Grind in a grinder or in a mortar and pestle.

3 Add salt to taste and serve.

Muj Chetin Doud Dhar

GRATED RADISH IN YOGHURT

Serves: 6

INGREDIENTS

500 gm / 1.1 lb Radish (*mooli*), washed, scraped,
  grated, squeezed
½ cup / 110 gm / 3½ oz Yoghurt (*dahi*), whisked
3 Green chillies, deseeded, cut into small pieces
Salt to taste
½ tsp Black cumin (*shah jeera*) seeds

METHOD

In a bowl, mix yoghurt, radish, green chillies,
and salt together. Sprinkle black cumin seeds and
serve.

Note: This can be served as a side dish any time.
If you want it spicy, add ½ tsp red chilli powder.

Gurdol Chetin

PLUM CHUTNEY

Serves: 6

INGREDIENTS

500 gm / 1.1 lb Plum (*gurdol*), deseeded
½ tsp / 1½ gm Red chilli powder
Salt to taste

METHOD

1 Put plum, red chilli powder, and salt in a mixer.
   Grind for a second.

2 Enjoy this chutney with any thing of
   your choice.

Aalch Chetin

SOUR CHERRY CHUTNEY

Serves: 6

INGREDIENTS

1 cup Cherries, deseeded, washed
Salt to taste
½ tsp / 1½ gm Red chilli powder

METHOD

1 Crush the cherries with your hands and remove
   the seeds.

2 Add salt and red chilli powder. Mix well.

3 Serve with steamed rice, chapati, *nan* or
   even pulao.

Doon Chetin

WALNUT CHUTNEY

Serves: 6

INGREDIENTS

1 cup / 120 gm / 4 oz Walnuts (*akhrot*), shelled,
  soaked in warm water for 2 hours, skin peeled
4 Green chillies
2 cups / 450 gm / 1 lb Yoghurt (*dahi*)
Salt to taste
½ tsp / 1¼ gm Black cumin (*shah jeera*) seeds

METHOD

1 Grind walnuts and green chillies to a fine
   paste.

2 Mix yoghurt and salt in a bowl. Add the walnut
   paste and mix well.

3 Refrigerate for 30 minutes before serving.

Note: This can be used as a dip for cocktail salads.

Buzith Nadir Chetin

ROASTED LOTUS STEM CHUTNEY

Serves: 6

INGREDIENTS

500 gm / 1.1 lb Lotus stems (*kamal kakri*), cut
  into 5 cm pieces, washed
1 Onion, medium-sized, chopped
2 Green chillies, deseeded
Salt to taste
$^1/_3$ cup Tamarind (*imli*) liquid
2 Lemon (*nimbu*) juice

METHOD

1 Roast the lotus stems on the gas or in a
   microwave. Grill for 10 minutes on each side.

2 Grind the lotus stems with onion, green chillies,
   and salt. Add lemon juice or tamarind liquid;
   mix well and serve.

Facing page: Autumn time, Dal Lake.
Photograph: S. Irfan

Talith Muj Chetin

FRIED RADISH CHUTNEY

Serves: 6

INGREDIENTS

1 kg / 2.2 lb Radish (*mooli*), washed, scraped, grated
3 tbsp / 45 ml / 1½ fl oz Mustard / Refined oil
Salt to taste
$^1/_3$ tsp Asafoetida (*hing*)
2 tsp / 6 gm Red chilli powder
1 tsp / 3 gm Ginger powder (*sonth*)
1 tsp / 2½ gm Black cumin (*shah jeera*) seeds
5 Dried red chillies (*sookhi lal mirch*), deseeded
½ tsp / 1½ gm *Ver* masala (see p. 16)

METHOD

1 Squeeze the water out from the grated radish.

2 Heat the oil in a pan; add salt, asafoetida, and grated radish. Keep stirring until the remaining water dries up. Add red chilli powder and ginger powder; fry for a minute. Sprinkle black cumin seeds, dried red chillies, and *ver* masala; mix well.

3 Enjoy the chutney with chapatti, rice or *nan*.

Note: Serve this chutney with haak *or any green vegetables.*

Sabz Badam Aanchar

GREEN ALMOND PICKLE

Serves: 6

INGREDIENTS

1 kg / 2.2 lb Green baby almonds (*badam*), washed, pat-dried
1 cup / 220 ml / 7 fl oz Mustard oil
3 tsp / 9 gm Black mustard (*rai*) seeds
Salt to taste
3 tsp / 9 gm Red chilli powder

METHOD

1 Mix oil, black mustard seeds, salt, and red chilli powder together in a pot.

2 Add green almonds and mix.

3 Put in an airtight jar and keep in the sun for a week.

4 Serve with all kinds of meals, vegetarian or non-vegetarian.

Note: This pickle is a delicacy of Kashmir cuisine.

Wazul Saboot Marchwangen Aanchar

WHOLE RED CHILLI PICKLE

Serves: 6-10

INGREDIENTS

1 kg / 2.2 lb Red chillies (*lal mirch*), fresh,
   washed, pat-dried
1 cup / 220 ml / 7 fl oz Mustard oil
3 tsp / 9 gm Red chilli powder
½ cup Black mustard seeds (*rai*)
Salt to taste

METHOD

1 Prick the chillies with a knife.

2 Mix all the spices and chillies together and put
   in a jar.

3 Tighten the jar and keep in the sun for a week
   and serve.

Snowfall in Srinagar.
Photograph: S. Irfan

Munj Aanchar

KNOL KHOL PICKLE

Serves: 6

INGREDIENT

1 kg / 2.2 lb Knol khol (*kholrabi*), washed
2 cups / 440 ml / 15 fl oz Mustard oil [raw]
5 tsp / 15 gm Red chilli powder
3 tsp / 9 gm Ginger powder (*sonth*)
1 cup Black mustard (*rai*) seeds
Salt to taste

METHOD

1 Separate the leaves from the balls of the knol khol and cut into 2-3 pieces each. Peel and cut the balls into 5-6 cm piece. Keep the knol khol and leaves to dry in the kitchen for 1 day in summer months and 2 days in winters so that the moisture evaporates totally. There should be no water left.

2 Put 2 cups of unheated mustard oil in a deep vessel. Add red chilli powder, ginger powder, and black mustard seeds, and salt. Add dried knol khol. Mix thoroughly till the spices are well mixed.

3 Transfer contents into an airtight jar. Keep in the sun for about a week.

4 Serve with non-vegetarian and vegetarian dishes.

Cher Aanchar

APRICOT PICKLE

Serves: 6

INGREDIENTS

1 kg / 2.2 lb Apricot (*khubani*), slightly hard to touch, washed, pat-dried
1½ cups / 330 ml / 11 fl oz Mustard Oil [raw]
3 tsp / 9 gm Red chilli powder
1 cup Black mustard (*rai*) seeds
Salt to taste

METHOD

1 Prick the apricots with a fork.

2 Mix oil, red chilli powder, black mustard seeds, and salt in a pot. Add apricot to the mixture and transfer into an airtight jar.

3 Keep the jar in the sun for 4-5 days.

4 Serve with any kind of dishes.

Note: This pickle is very typical of Kashmir. Make sure the apricot is not soft.

A view of the city enveloped by thick snow blanket.
Photograph: S. Irfan

A tea break in the field.
Photograph: Mukhtar Ahmad

DESSERTS

Kheer

RICE PUDDING

Serves: 6

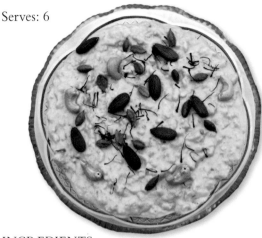

INGREDIENTS

½ cup / 100 gm / 3½ oz Basmati rice, soaked
  overnight
8 cups / 2 lt / 64 fl oz Full-cream milk, boiled
2 cups / 400 gm / 14 oz Sugar
¼ cup / 35 gm / 1¼ oz Almonds (*badam*),
  soaked, peeled
$^1/_3$ cup Raisins (*kishmish*)
¼ cup / 20 gm Dry coconut (*nariyal*), shredded
6 Cashew nuts (*kaju*), crushed
1 tsp Saffron (*kesar*)
5 Green cardamoms (*choti elaichi*), crushed

METHOD

1 Crush the soaked rice with your hands and put
  in a deep vessel. Pour 4 cups water and boil till
  the rice is mixed well with the water.

2 Add milk and boil, stirring continuously, till it
  is mixed well and the consistency is thick. Add
  sugar, keep mixing with a ladle.

3 Add all the dry fruits, saffron, and crushed
  green cardamom; mix well. Bring to the boil
  and simmer for 20 minutes. Remove and keep
  aside to cool.

4 Serve chilled.

Phirin

SEMOLINA GARNISHED WITH DRY FRUITS

Serves: 6

INGREDIENT

½ cup / 100 gm / 3½ oz Semolina (*suji*), soaked
  for 1 hour
4 cups / 1 lt / 32 fl oz Full-cream milk, boiled
½ cup / 100 gm / 3½ oz Sugar
2 tbsp Cashew nuts (*kaju*), crushed
6 Almonds (*badam*), soaked, peeled
2 tbsp Pistachios (*pista*), crushed
½ tsp Saffron (*kesar*)

METHOD

1 Boil semolina in 2 cups water till it is mixed
  well with water. Add milk and bring to the
  boil, stirring constantly.

2 Add dry fruits and saffron and boil till the
  mixture thickens. Simmer for 20 minutes
  stirring well. Remove and serve chilled.

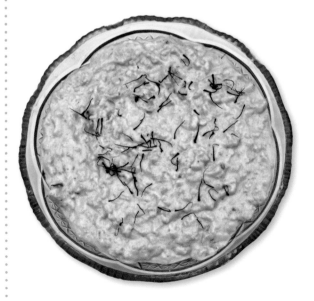

Shufta

SWEETENED COTTAGE CHEESE WITH DRY FRUITS

Serves: 6

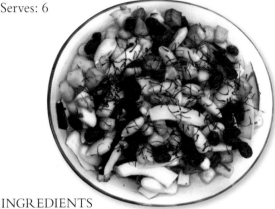

INGREDIENTS

250 gm / 9 oz Cottage cheese (*paneer*), cut into
½ cm cubes
½ cup / 110 ml / 3½ fl oz Refined oil / Ghee
1 cup / 200 gm / 7 oz Sugar
½ cup / 40 gm / 1¼ oz Coconut (*nariyal*), fresh,
chopped
½ cup / 70 gm / 2¾ oz Almonds (*badam*), peeled
½ cup / 70 gm / 2¾ oz Raisins (*kishmish*)
6 Green cardamoms (*choti elaichi*), crushed
½ tsp Saffron, soaked in 2 tsp warm water

METHOD

1 Heat the oil in a deep pan; deep-fry the cottage
cheese and keep aside.

2 Boil the sugar in 6 cups water. Add the fried
cottage cheese and boil for 5 more minutes.

3 Heat 1 tbsp oil in a frying pan; fry the coconut
and almonds for 1-2 minutes. Add to the
boiling cottage cheese. Add raisins, green
cardamoms and saffron extract and boil for
another 3 minutes. Remove and cool till room
temperature. Serve with the main course or as
a dessert.

*Note: This dish is cooked only on special
occasions like weddings, festivals, etc. This is Lata
Mangeshkar's favourite dish among many others.*

Top: Carrying earthenware in wicker baskets.
Below: Embroidering a shawl with Kashmiri motifs.

119

Sheer Chai

PINK SALTY TEA

Serves: 6

INGREDIENTS

1 tsp *Kehwa* tea leaves
¼ tsp Sodium bicarbonate
2 cups / 480 ml / 16 fl oz Milk
Salt to taste
2 tsp Cream of boiled milk
2 Almonds (*badam*), crushed
2 Green cardamoms (*choti elaichi*), crushed

METHOD

1 Boil 1 cup water, soda bicarbonate, and tea leaves in a pot for 10 minutes.

2 If the water starts drying up, add 1 more cup of water. Keep boiling till the colour of the tea turns dark.

3 Add 1 more cup of water, milk, and salt. Bring to the boil.

4 Strain into cups. Add little bit of cream on top, crushed almonds and green cardamom. Serve after meals.

Note: This tea acts as a digestive after a heavy meal.

Kehwa

KASHMIRI GREEN TEA

Serves: 6

INGREDIENTS

1 tsp *Kehwa* tea leaves, crushed
Sugar to taste
4 Green cardamoms (*choti elaichi*), crushed
1 tsp / 3 gm Cinnamon (*dalchini*) powder
6 Almonds (*badam*), crushed

METHOD

1 Boil 6 cups water in a pot. Add sugar to taste followed by tea leaves.

2 Add crushed green cardamom and cinnamon powder; mix well.

3 Strain the mixture into individual tea cups.

4 Sprinkle crushed almonds on the cups and serve.

Note: Traditionally this tea is served after dinner and at breakfast. It is very good for curing cough and cold and can be enjoyed anytime.

Facing page: The backwaters of Srinagar about a 100 years ago.

*Hari Parbat Fort in Srinagar on top with the famous
Hazrat Makhdoom Sahib Shrine on the left. This shrine
attracts thousands of pilgrims everyday as it is reputed for
its healing power.*
Photograph: Mukhtar Ahmad

LOW CALORIE RECIPES

Varimooth t, Gogje

BLACK KIDNEY BEANS WITH TURNIPS

Serves: 6-8

INGREDIENTS

1 kg / 2.2 lb Black kidney beans, soaked
   overnight, drained
4-6 pieces Turnips (*shalgam*), peeled, washed, cut
   into 4-6 pieces
1 tbsp / 15 ml Mustard oil
½ tsp Asafoetida (*hing*)
Salt to taste
3 tsp / 9 gm Red chilli powder
2 tsp / 6 gm Ginger powder (*sonth*)
2 tsp / 6 gm *Ver* masala (see p. 16)
5 Dried red chillies (*sookhi lal mirch*)

METHOD

1 Heat the oil in a pressure cooker; add asafoetida,
salt, 20 cups water, kidney beans, red chilli
powder, and ginger powder. Pressure cook for
5 minutes.

2 Open the lid and add turnips and pressure cook
again for 5 minutes. Let it cool down, add *ver*
masala, stir well and boil till the turnips and
beans are tender. (The gravy in this dish should
be thin.)

Olav Dude Legit

POTATOES IN YOGHURT

Serves: 6

INGREDIENTS

1 kg / 1.1 lb Potatoes, peeled, washed, cut into
   1″-thick, round pieces
1 cup / 225 gm / 8 oz Yoghurt (*dahi*), whisked
1 tbsp / 15 ml Refined oil
2 Cloves (*laung*)
1 Bay leaf (*tej patta*)
2 tsp / 6 gm Turmeric (*haldi*) powder
2 tsp / 6 gm Ginger powder (*sonth*)
2 tsp / 4 gm Cumin (*jeera*) seeds
Salt to taste
1 tsp / 2½ gm Black cumin (*shah jeera*) seeds

METHOD

1 Heat the oil in a deep vessel; add potatoes,
cloves, and bay leaf. Fry for 5 minutes. Add
4 cups water, turmeric powder, ginger powder,
cumin seeds, and salt; cook till the potatoes are
tender.

2 Add yoghurt and mix well. Add black cumin
seeds and simmer for 2 minutes.

3 Serve the way you like.

T Chat Gogje

TURNIPS IN LIGHT GRAVY

Serves: 6

INGREDIENTS

1 kg / 2.2 lb Turnips (*shalgam*), peeled, washed, sliced
1 tbsp / 15 ml Refined oil
¼ tsp Asafoetida (*hing*)
Salt to taste
5 Dried red chillies (*sookhi lal mirch*)
½ tsp / 1½ gm *Ver* masala (see p. 16)

METHOD

1 Heat the oil in a pressure cooker; add asafoetida, salt, and turnips; stir. Add ½ cup water and pressure cook for 10 minutes.

2 Open the lid and pour 4 cups water. Add dried red chillies and *ver* masala; cook on high heat till the gravy thickens.

3 Serve hot.

Gogje t, Nadir

TURNIPS WITH LOTUS STEMS

Serves: 6

INGREDIENTS

1 kg / 2.2 lb Turnips (*shalgam*), peeled, washed, shredded
500 gm / 1.1 lb Lotus stems (*kamal kakri*), scraped, washed, cut into horizontal pieces
1 tbsp / 15 ml Mustard / Refined oil
¼ tsp Asafoetida (*hing*)
Salt to taste
4 Dried red chillies (*sookhi lal mirch*), deseeded
1 tsp / 3 gm *Ver* masala (see p. 16)

METHOD

1 Heat the oil in a pressure cooker; add asafoetida, salt, turnips, and lotus stems. Pour ½ cup water, mix well and pressure cook for 5 minutes.

2 Open the lid and cook on high heat, stirring occasionally. Add 4 cups water and dried red chillies, cook till both the turnips and lotus stems are tender.

3 Add *ver* masala and mix well.

4 Serve hot.

Potters working on heavy wheel!

Phool t, Nadir

CAULIFLOWER WITH LOTUS STEMS

Serves: 6

INGREDIENTS

1 kg / 2.2 lb Cauliflower (*phool gobi*), cut into
  florets, washed, drained
250 gm / 9 oz Lotus stems (*kamal kakri*), scraped,
  washed, cut into 2″-long pieces
1 tbsp / 15 ml Refined oil
½ tsp Asafoetida (*hing*)
Salt to taste
3 tsp / 9 gm Red chilli powder
2 tsp / 6 gm Ginger powder (*sonth*)
1 tsp / 2 gm Cumin (*jeera*) seeds

METHOD

1 Heat the oil in a pressure cooker; add asafoetida,
  salt, cauliflower, and lotus stems. Cook on high
  heat for 5 minutes. Add red chilli powder,
  ginger powder, cumin seeds, and ½ cup water;
  pressure cook for 5 minutes or till one whistle.

2 Open the lid quickly and your dish is ready
  to serve.

Moung Dal Dhulee

SIMPLE GREEN GRAM

Serves: 6

INGREDIENTS

2½ cups / 500 gm / 1.1 lb Green gram (*moong
  dal*), washed
½ tsp Refined oil
¼ tsp Asafoetida (*hing*)
Salt to taste
1 tsp / 3 gm Turmeric (*haldi*) powder
1 tsp / 3 gm Ginger powder (*sonth*)
1 tsp / 2 gm Cumin (*jeera*) seeds
4 Green chillies

METHOD

1 Heat the oil in a deep pot; add asafoetida, salt,
  6 cups water, turmeric powder, ginger powder,
  and cumin seeds. Cook on high heat till the
  lentil is well mixed and soft.

2 Add green chillies and simmer for 5 minutes.
  Remove.

3 Serve with steamed rice, chapatti or *nan*.

Chana Dal
FLAVOURED BENGAL GRAM

Serves: 6

INGREDIENTS

2½ cups / 500 gm / 1.1 lb Bengal gram (*chana
  dal*), washed, soaked for 1 hour
1 tsp / 5 ml Refined oil
½ tsp Asafoetida (*hing*)
Salt to taste
1 tsp / 3 gm Turmeric (*haldi*) powder
2 tsp / 6 gm Ginger powder (*sonth*)
1 tsp / 2 gm Cumin (*jeera*) seeds
1 tsp / 3 gm Fennel (*saunf*) powder
4 Green chillies

METHOD

1 Heat the oil in a pressure cooker; add asafoetida,
   salt, 6 cups water, turmeric powder, ginger
   powder, cumin powder, fennel powder, and
   Bengal gram. Pressure cook for 15 minutes.

2 Open the lid and check if the Bengal gram is
   tender and mixed well.

3 Remove and garnish with green chillies.
   Serve hot.

Moung Dal Chilka t, Gogje
GREEN SPLIT LENTILS WITH TURNIPS

Serves: 6

INGREDIENTS

2½ cups / 500 gm / 1.1 lb Green gram (*moong
  dal*), split
250 gm / 9 oz Turnips (*shalgam*), peeled, washed,
  cut into 6″ pieces
1 tbsp / 15 ml Mustard oil
½ tsp Asafoetida (*hing*)
Salt to taste
1 tsp / 3 gm Turmeric (*haldi*) powder
1 tsp / 3 gm Ginger powder (*sonth*)
2 tsp / 6 gm Fennel (*saunf*) powder
5 Dried red chillies (*sookhi lal mirch*)

METHOD

1 Heat the oil in a pressure cooker; add asafoetida,
   salt, 8 cups water, turmeric powder, ginger
   powder, fennel powder, green gram, and
   turnips. Pressure cook for 10 minutes.

2 Open the lid and add dried red chillies. Cook for
   5 minutes and serve hot.

A man walks amidst heavy snowfall in Srinagar.
Photograph: S. Irfan

Moung Dal t, Muj

WHOLE GREEN LENTIL WITH RADISH

Serves: 6

INGREDIENTS

1 kg / 2.2 lb Whole Green gram (*moong dal*),
  soaked for 15 minutes
500 gm / 1.1 lb Radish (*mooli*), peeled, cut into
  3″ pieces
Salt to taste
½ tsp Asafoetida (*hing*)
2 tsp / 6 gm Turmeric (*haldi*) powder
2 tsp / 6 gm Ginger powder (*sonth*)
3 tsp / 9 gm Fennel (*saunf*) powder
1 tsp / 2 gm Cumin (*jeera*) seeds
4 Dried red chillies (*sookhi lal mirch*)
1 tbsp / 15 ml Mustard oil (optional)

METHOD

1 Heat the oil in a pressure cooker; add radish and
  fry for 2 minutes.

2 Add soaked green gram along with 8 cups
  water, salt, asafoetida, turmeric powder, ginger
  powder, fennel powder, and cumin seeds; stir
  and pressure cook for 10 minutes.

3 Remove from heat, open the lid when it cools
  down. Return to heat and bring the mixture to
  the boil. Add dried red chillies and serve hot.

Moung Dal t, Nadir

WHOLE GREEN LENTIL WITH LOTUS STEMS

Serves: 6-8

INGREDIENTS

1 kg / 2.2 lb Whole Green gram (*moong dal*),
  soaked for 15 minutes
500 gm / 1.1 lb Lotus stems (*kamal kakri*),
  scraped, cut into 3″-long pieces, cleaned under
  tap water
2 tsp / 6 gm Turmeric (*haldi*) powder
2 tsp / 6 gm Ginger powder (*sonth*)
3 tsp / 9 gm Fennel (*saunf*) powder
Salt to taste
½ tsp Asafoetida (*hing*)
2 tsp / 4 gm Cumin (*jeera*) seeds
5 Dried red chillies (*sookhi lal mirch*), deseeded
1 tsp / 5 ml Mustard oil, optional

METHOD

1 Add soaked green gram in a pressure cooker
  with 8 cups water, lotus stems, oil, turmeric
  powder, ginger powder, fennel powder, salt,
  asafoetida, and cumin seeds; mix well with a
  ladle and pressure cook for 10 minutes.

2 After it cools down open the lid of cooker and
  bring the mixture to the boil till it is mixed well.

3 Add dried red chillies and boil for 2 minutes.
  Serve hot.

Ruins of a temple at Martand.

128

Muj Mulvin

RADISH GREENS

Serves: 6

INGREDIENTS

1 kg / 2.2 lb Radish (*mooli*) with leaves, leaves
  cut and cleaned, radish scraped and sliced
1 tbsp / 15 ml Mustard oil
¼ tsp Asafoetida (*hing*)
Salt to taste
4 Dried red chillies (*sookhi lal mirch*)
½ tsp *Ver* masala (see p. 16)

METHOD

1 Put 4 cups water in a pressure cooker. Add
radish and leaves together; pressure cook for
15 minutes.

2 Open the lid and drain the water out. Wash
under a tap and squeeze properly.

3 Heat the oil in a deep pot; add asafoetida, salt,
and the radish with leaves. Stir well and pour 6
cups water. Bring to the boil and add dried red
chillies and *ver* masala; mix well.

4 Serve hot with steamed rice

Razma Hembh t, Nadir

STIR FRIED FRENCH BEANS WITH LOTUS STEMS

Serves: 6

INGREDIENTS

1 kg / 2.2 lb French beans, stringed, cut into 2,
  washed
200 gm / 7 oz Lotus stems (*kamal kakri*), scraped,
  cut into ½″-thick rounds, washed thoroughly
2 tbsp / 30 ml / 1 fl oz Mustard / Refined /
  Olive oil
Salt to taste
¼ tsp Asafoetida (*hing*)
1 tsp / 2 gm Cumin (*jeera*) seeds
2 tsp / 6 gm Red chilli powder
1 tsp / 3 gm Ginger powder (*sonth*)
3 Dried red chillies (*sookhi lal mirch*), deseeded

METHOD

1 Heat the oil in a pan; add salt, asafoetida, cumin
seeds, French beans, and lotus stems. Stir and
cook on high heat for 5 minutes. Add red
chilli powder and ginger powder; mix well and
simmer for 15 minutes, stirring occasionally till
the beans and lotus stems are tender.

2 Add the dried red chillies and mix.

3 Serve with chapatti or any thing of your choice.

Hedder Yakhni

MUSHROOMS IN YOGHURT

Serves: 6

INGREDIENTS

1 kg / 2.2 lb Mushroom, cut into half, washed
2 cups / 450 gm / 1 lb Yoghurt (*dahi*), whisked
1 tsp / 5 ml Mustard / Refined / Olive oil
2 Bay leaves (*tej patta*)
2 Cloves (*laung*)
1 Cinnamon (*dalchini*) stick
Salt to taste
3 tsp / 9 gm Fennel (*saunf*) powder
2 tsp / 6 gm Ginger powder (*sonth*)
1 tsp / 2½ gm Black cumin (*shah jeera*) seeds

METHOD

1 Boil the mushrooms in 3 cups water for 5 minutes; drain well.

2 Heat the oil in a deep pot; add bay leaves, cloves, cinnamon stick, and salt. Add mushrooms and fry for 5 minutes.

3 Add 4 cups water, fennel powder, and ginger powder. Cook for 2 minutes. Add yoghurt and mix well; cook till the gravy thickens.

4 Sprinkle black cumin seeds and serve hot.

Note: Do not add water in this vegetable. It is cooked in its own moisture, tastes delicious and is high in fibre.

Razma Hembh t, Gand

FRENCH BEANS WITH ONIONS

Serves: 6

INGREDIENTS

1 kg / 2.2 lb French beans, stringed, cut into 2, washed
200 gm / 7 oz Onions, peeled, cut into
2 tbsp / 30 ml / 1 fl oz Mustard / Refined / Olive oil
Salt to taste
¼ tsp Asafoetida (*hing*)
2 tsp / 6 gm Red chilli powder
1 tsp / 3 gm Ginger powder (*sonth*)
1 tsp / 2 gm Cumin (*jeera*) seeds
5 Dried red chillies (*sookhi lal mirch*), deseeded

METHOD

1 Heat the oil in a pan; add salt, asafoetida, beans, and onions. Stir on high heat for 5 minutes. Simmer and add red chilli powder, ginger powder, and cumin seeds. Mix well.

2 Add dried red chillies and simmer till the beans are tender.

3 Serve with chapatti, *nan,* or any thing of your choice.

Note: Cook this vegetable on low heat and without any water as it cooks in its own miosture.

Chaman Kaliya

COTTAGE CHEESE IN YELLOW GRAVY

Serves: 6-8

INGREDIENTS

1 kg / 2.2 lb Cottage cheese (*paneer*), cut into
  1″-thick, square pieces
1 tbsp / 15 ml Mustard / Refined / Olive oil
1 Bay leaf (*tej patta*)
1 Cinnamon (*dalchini*) stick
2 Cloves (*laung*)
Salt to taste
2 tsp / 6 gm Turmeric (*haldi*) powder
2 tsp / 6 gm Ginger powder (*sonth*)
3 tsp / 9 gm Fennel (*saunf*) powder
1 tsp / 3 gm Cumin (*jeera*) powder
1 cup / 240 ml / 8 fl oz Milk, skimmed, boiled
4 Green cardamom (*choti elaichi*), crushed

METHOD

1 Heat the oil in a deep pot; add bay leaf, cinnamon
   stick, cloves, salt, and 8 cups water. Bring to the
   boil and add turmeric powder, ginger powder,
   fennel powder, and cumin powder; mix well.

2 Add cottage cheese and cook till the cheese is
   soft and the gravy thickens.

3 Add milk and cook for 2 minutes. Sprinkle
   crushed green cardamom and mix well.

4 Serve hot.

*Note: This dish is low in calories because the cottage
cheese is not fried which is normally done. And the oil
used is only 1 tsp. Cottage cheese is a good source of
calcium.*

Left: Dal Lake
*Right: A break on a long journey about a 100 years
ago.*

131

Gole AI t, Dooen Gooje
PUMPKIN WITH WALNUTS

Serves: 6

INGREDIENTS

1 kg / 2.2 lb Pumpkin (*kaddu*), peeled, cut into cubes, washed, drained
¾ cup / 100 gm / 3½ oz Walnuts (*akhrot*), soaked, peeled
2 tbsp / 30 ml / 1 fl oz Mustard / Refined / Olive oil
Salt to taste
1 tsp / 3 gm Turmeric (*haldi*) powder
4 Dried red chillies (*sookhi lal mirch*), deseeded

METHOD

1 Heat the oil in a pressure cooker; add pumpkin and salt, stir. Pressure cook for 10 minutes.

2 Open the lid and mix well; cook on high heat. Add turmeric powder and keep stirring till the water dries up.

3 Add walnuts and dried red chillies; mix well.

4 Serve hot.

Mattar t, Gand
PEAS WITH ONIONS

Serves: 6

INGREDIENTS

1 kg / 2.2 lb Green peas (*hara mattar*), fresh or frozen
250 gm / 9 oz Onions, peeled, chopped
1 tbsp / 15 ml Refined / Olive oil
Salt to taste
1 tsp / 2 gm Cumin (*jeera*) seeds
2 tsp / 6 gm Red chilli powder
2 tsp / 6 gm Ginger powder (*sonth*)

METHOD

1 Heat the oil in a pressure cooker; add onions, salt, and cumin seeds. Fry for 2 minutes. Add peas and stir for 2 minutes. Add red chilli powder, ginger powder, and ½ cup water; pressure cook for 2 minutes.

2 Open the lid and serve hot.

The scented saffron flower.
Photograph: Mukhtar Ahmad

Bandh Gupi t, Tamatar

CABBAGE COOKED WITH TOMATOES

Serves: 6

INGREDIENTS

1 kg / 2.2 lb Cabbage (*bandh gobi*), cut into large
single pieces, washed, drained
1 cup Tomatoes, chopped
2 tbsp / 30 ml / 1 fl oz Mustard / Refined /
Olive oil
Salt to taste
¼ tsp Asafoetida (*hing*)
1 tsp / 2 gm Cumin (*jeera*) seeds
2 tsp / 6 gm Red chilli powder
2 tsp / 6 gm Ginger powder (*sonth*)
1 tsp / 3 gm *Ver* masala (see p. 16)

METHOD

1 Heat the oil in a pressure cooker; add salt,
asafoetida, cumin seeds, and cabbage. Cook
on high heat for 5 minutes; add tomatoes
and mix well. Add red chilli powder
and ginger powder; pressure cook for
5 minutes.

2 Remove from heat, open the lid and check if the
cabbage is tender. Return to heat and simmer
for 5 minutes. Add *ver* masala; mix well.

3 Serve hot.

Bandh Gupi t, Nadir

CABBAGE WITH LOTUS STEMS

Serves: 6

INGREDIENTS

1 kg / 2.2 lb Cabbage (*bandh gobi*), washed, cut
into medium-sized pieces
250 gm / 9 oz Lotus stems (*kamal kakri*), scraped,
cut into small round pieces, washed, drained
2 tbsp / 30 ml / 1 fl oz Mustard / Refined /
Olive oil
¼ tsp Asafoetida (*hing*)
Salt to taste
1 tsp / 2 gm Cumin (*jeera*) seeds
2 tsp / 6 gm Red chilli powder
1 tsp / 3 gm Ginger powder (*sonth*)
1 tsp / 3 gm *Ver* masala (see p. 16)
5 Dried red chillies (*sookhi lal mirch*), deseeded

METHOD

1 Heat the oil in a pressure cooker; add asafoetida,
salt, cumin seeds, cabbage, and lotus stems. Mix
well with a ladle. Pour 1 cup water and add red
chilli powder, ginger powder, and *ver* masala.
Pressure cook for 5 minutes.

2 Remove from heat and open the lid. Add dried
red chillies and mix.

3 Serve hot.

Ladakhis

133

Razma t, Gogje
KIDNEY BEANS WITH TURNIPS

Serves: 6

INGREDIENTS

1 kg / 2.2 lb Kidney beans (*rajma*), soaked
  overnight, drained
250 gm / 9 oz Turnips (*shalgam*), peeled, washed,
  cut into 4 pieces
½ tsp Asafoetida (hing)
Salt to taste
3 tsp / 9 gm Red chilli powder
2 tsp / 6 gm Ginger powder (*sonth*)
2 tsp / 6 gm *Ver* masala (see p. 16)

METHOD

1 Pressure cook soaked beans in 15 cups fresh
   water for 5 minutes.

2 Open the lid, add turnip, asafoetida, salt, red
   chilli powder, and ginger powder; mix well.
   Again pressure cook for 5 minutes.

3 Add *ver* masala and bring to the boil.

4 Serve with rice or anything of your choice.

Kokur t, Tureel
CHICKEN WITH SNAKE GOURD

Serves: 6

INGREDIENTS

1 kg / 2.2 lb Chicken, boneless or with bones,
  washed
2 kg / 4.4 lb Snake gourd (*turai*), scraped, cut into
  medium-sized pieces, washed
2 tbsp / 30 ml / 1 fl oz Mustard oil / Refined /
  Olive oil
Salt to taste
½ tsp Asafoetida (*hing*)
1 tsp / 2 gm Cumin (*jeera*) seeds
2 tsp / 6 gm Turmeric (*haldi*) powder
3 tsp / 9 gm Fennel (*saunf*) powder
2 tsp / 6 gm Ginger powder (*sonth*)
1 tsp / 3 gm Cumin powder

METHOD

1 Heat the oil in a deep pot; add salt, asafoetida,
   cumin seeds, and chicken. Stir for 10 minutes
   on high heat. Add snake gourd and mix well.
   Add all the powdered spices and 4 cups water;
   stir and cook till the gravy is thick and chicken
   is tender.

2 Serve garnished with green chillies and
   accompanied with steamed rice or chapatti.

Kokur Yakhni

CHICKEN IN YOGHURT

Serves: 6

INGREDIENTS

1 kg / 2.2 lb Chicken, leg and thigh pieces
3 cups / 675 gm / 24 oz Yoghurt (*dahi*), whisked
  made of skimmed milk
2 tbsp / 30 ml / 1 fl oz Mustard / Refined /
  Olive oil
½ tsp Asafoetida (*hing*)
Salt to taste
2 Bay leaves (*tej patta*)
2 Cloves (*laung*)
2 Cinnamon (*dalchini*) sticks
2 tsp / 6 gm Ginger powder (*sonth*)
3 tsp / 9 gm Fennel (*saunf*) powder
1 tsp / 3 gm Cumin (*jeera*) powder
5 Green cardamoms (*choti elaichi*), crushed
2 Black cardamoms (*badi elaichi*), crushed
1 tsp / 2½ gm Black cumin (*shah jeera*) seeds

METHOD

1 Heat the oil in a deep vessel; add asafoetida,
  salt, bay leaves, cloves, cinnamon sticks, and
  chicken; stir for 10 minutes. Add 6 cups water,
  ginger powder, fennel powder, and cumin
  powder; cook till the chicken is tender. Remove
  from heat.

2 Transfer the gravy from the cooked chicken into
  a separate pot. Add yoghurt and bring to the
  boil; stirring well. Add crushed green and black
  cardamoms and sprinkle black cumin seeds;
  mix well.

3 Pour this gravy back into the chicken and bring
  to the boil. Remove.

4 Serve hot.

Kokur Kaliya

CHICKEN KALIYA

Serves: 6

INGREDIENTS

1 kg / 2.2 lb Chicken, cut into 12 pieces, washed
1 tbsp / 15 ml Mustard / Refined / Olive oil
½ tsp Asafoetida (*hing*)
Salt to taste
2 Cloves (*laung*)
2 Bay leaves (*tej patta*)
2 Cinnamon (*dalchini*) sticks
2 tsp / 6 gm Ginger powder (*sonth*)
1½ tsp / 4½ gm Turmeric (*haldi*) powder
3 tsp / 9 gm Fennel (*saunf*) powder
2 tsp / 4 gm Cumin (*jeera*) seeds
1 cup / 240 ml / 8 fl oz Skimmed milk (boiled)
4 Green cardamoms (*choti elaichi*), crushed
2 Black cardamoms (*badi elaichi*), crushed

METHOD

1 Heat the oil in a deep pot; add asafoetida, salt,
  cloves, bay leaves, cinnamon sticks, and chicken.
  Stir for 5 minutes. Add 6 cups water, ginger
  powder, turmeric powder, fennel powder, and
  cumin seeds; cook on high heat till the chicken
  is tender.

2 Add milk and bring
  to the boil. Add
  crushed green
  and black
  cardamoms;
  mix.

3 Serve hot.

The Dal Lake famous for its houseboats and shikhars is surrounded by the snow-capped mountains.
Photograph: Mukhtar Ahmad

Buzith Kokur

GRILLED CHICKEN

Serves: 6

INGREDIENTS

1 kg / 2.2 lb Chicken, leg and thigh pieces,
  washed, drained
1 cup / 225 gm / 8 oz Yoghurt (*dahi*)
Salt to taste
2 tsp / 12 gm Ginger (*adrak*) paste
2 tsp / 12 gm Garlic (*lasan*) paste
2 tsp / 6 gm Cumin (*jeera*) powder
2 tsp / 6 gm Red chilli powder
1 tbsp / 15 ml Olive oil

METHOD

1 In a bowl, mix yoghurt, salt, ginger and garlic
   pastes, cumin powder, red chilli powder, olive
   oil, and chicken together. Marinate for 2 hours.

2 Preheat oven to 180°C / 350°F and grill the
   chicken till golden brown, or grill in the
   microwave.

3 Serve with chapatti or *nan*.

A chilly winter evening by the Dal Lake.
Photograph: S. Irfan

Kokur Kabab

CHICKEN KEBAB

Serves: 6

INGREDIENTS

1 kg / 2.2 lb Chicken mince, done 4 times in
  mixer
Salt to taste
2 tsp / 12 gm Ginger (*adrak*) paste
1 tsp / 6 gm Garlic (*lasan*) paste
3 tsp / 9 gm Red chilli powder
1 tsp / 2½ gm Black cumin (*shah jeera*) seeds
2 tsp / 6 gm Black cardamoms (*badi elaichi*)
  powder
4 Green chillies, chopped
1 tbsp / 15 ml Refined oil
$^{1}/_{3}$ cup Green coriander (*hara dhaniya*) leaves,
  chopped
2 tbsp Dry mint leaves

METHOD

1 Put the mince in a bowl. Add salt, ginger paste,
   garlic paste, red chilli powder, cumin seeds,
   black cardamom powder, green chillies, and
   oil; mix well with your hands.

2 Divide the mixture into equal portions and
   mould one portion on a skewer pressing with
   your palm and finger shaping into a sausage.
   Grill on charcoal fire or in microwave oven for
   10 minutes, turning around carefully. Repeat
   till all are grilled.

Kokur Shyami

CHICKEN CUTLETS IN YOGHURT

Serves: 6-8

INGREDIENTS

1 kg / 2.2 lb Chicken mince
2 tsp / 6 gm Ginger powder (*sonth*)
3 tsp / 9 gm Fennel (*saunf*) powder
2 tsp / 4 gm Cumin (*jeera*) seeds
Salt to taste
2 tsp / 6 gm Black cardamoms (*badi elaichi*)
  powder [for mixing]
2 tbsp / 30 ml / 1 fl oz Refined oil
3 Cloves (*laung*)
2 Cinnamon (*dalchini*) sticks
2 Bay leaves (*tej patta*)
3 cups / 675 gm / 24 oz Yoghurt (*dahi*), made of
  skimmed milk, whisked
2 tsp / 5 gm Black cumin (*shah jeera*) seeds
3 Black cardamoms, crushed
4 Green cardamoms (*choti elaichi*), crushed

METHOD

1 Put the mince in a bowl. Add 1 tsp ginger powder, 1 tsp fennel powder, 1 tsp cumin seeds, ½ tsp salt, and black cardamom powder; mix well.

2 Divide the mixture into equal portions and shape into 2″-long and 1″-thick, round cutlets.

3 Heat the oil in a large pot; add cloves, cinnamon sticks, bay leaves, and 6 cups water. Bring to the boil. Add the remaining spices and boil. Add cutlets and cook on high heat till the gravy thickens.

4 Add yoghurt and cook, stirring occasionally, till the gravy thickens.

5 Garnish with black cumin seeds and crushed black and green cardamoms. Serve hot.

Buzith Kabargah

GRILLED LAMB CHUNKS

Serves: 6

INGREDIENTS

1 kg / 2.2 lb Lamb, cut from breast in squares,
  washed
2 cups / 480 ml / 15 fl oz Skimmed milk, boiled
1 Bay leaf (*tej patta*)
1 Cinnamon (*dalchini*) stick
2 Cloves (*laung*)
4 Green cardamoms (*choti elaichi*), crushed
2 Black cardamoms (*badi elaichi*), crushed
¼ tsp Fennel (*saunf*) powder
1 tsp / 3 gm Ginger powder (*sonth*)
1 tsp / 3 gm Cumin (*jeera*) powder
Salt to taste
¼ tsp Saffron (*kesar*) extract

METHOD

1 In a pressure cooker, add the meat, 2 cups water, milk, bay leaf, cinnamon stick, cloves, crushed green and brown cardamom, fennel powder, ginger powder, cumin powder, salt, and saffron. Pressure cook for 10 minutes.

2 Remove from heat and check if the meat is tender. Cook on high heat again till the gravy is absorbed completely.

3 Take out the meat pieces with a tong carefully so that they do not break.

4 Preheat oven to 180°C / 350°F and grill the meat till golden brown or in a microwave, grill for 20 minutes on each side turning carefully.

5 Serve hot and decorate on a bed of lettuce.

Bandh T, Syun

CABBAGE WITH MEAT

Serves: 6

INGREDIENTS

1 kg / 2.2 lb Lamb, cut from shoulder
1 kg / 2.2 lb Cabbage (*bandh gobi*), cut into full
   pieces, washed well
2 tbsp / 30 ml / 1 fl oz Mustard / Refined oil
½ tsp Asafoetida (*hing*)
Salt to taste
1 tsp / 2 gm Cumin (*jeera*) seeds
2 tsp / 6 gm Turmeric (*haldi*) powder
2 tsp / 6 gm Ginger powder (*sonth*)
3 tsp / 9 gm Fennel (*saunf*) powder
1 tsp / 3 gm Cumin powder
5 Green chillies

METHOD

1 Heat the oil in a pressure cooker; add asafoetida,
   salt, cumin seeds, and lamb. Cook on high heat
   for 10 minutes. Pressure cook for 5 minutes.

2 Open the lid, add cabbage, mix well with a
   ladle and cook on high heat. Add 4 cups water
   and all the powdered spices; stir well. Pressure
   cook for 5 minutes.

3 Serve garnished with green chillies.

*The Shalimar Garden was built for Nur Jahan by her
husband Jehangir in 1616. The top most of the four
terraces called the 'Abode of Love' was reserved for the
emperor and the ladies of court.*

Buzith Syun

GRILLED LAMB

Serves: 6

INGREDIENTS

1 kg / 2.2 lb Lamb, cut from leg
1 cup / 225 gm / 8 oz Yoghurt (*dahi*)
2 tsp / 12 gm Garlic (*lasan*) paste
2 tsp / 12 gm Ginger (*adrak*) paste
1 tbsp / 15 ml Olive / Refined oil
Salt to taste
2 tsp / 6 gm Red chilli powder
1 tsp / 3 gm Cumin (*jeera*) powder
3 tbsp / 45 gm / 1½ oz Papaya paste
1 tbsp / 15 ml Cooking vinegar

METHOD

1 In a deep bowl, mix yoghurt with garlic and
   ginger pastes, oil, salt, red chilli powder, cumin
   powder, papaya paste, and vinegar; mix well.

2 Add lamb mix well and marinate for 12 hours.

3 Preheat the oven to 180°C / 350°F and grill
   the lamb till golden brown. Or grill in the
   microwave oven till golden brown.

Buzith Mach

GRILLED LAMB CUTLETS

Serves: 6

INGREDIENTS

1 kg / 2.2 lb Minced lamb
1 tbsp / 15 gm Yoghurt (*dahi*)
2 tsp / 6 gm Red chilli powder
1 tsp / 3 gm Ginger powder (*sonth*)
2 tsp / 6 gm Cumin (*jeera*) powder
Salt to taste
1 tbsp / 15 ml Mustard oil

METHOD

1 In a deep bowl, mix yoghurt, minced meat, red chilli powder, ginger powder, cumin powder, salt, and oil together; mix well and marinate for 1 hour.

2 Divide the mixture into equal portions and shape into round or rectangular cutlets.

3 Grill the cutlets in a microwave till brown or grill in a preheated oven at 180°C / 350°F till brown.

4 Serve as a snack or with the main course.

Buzith Gaad

GRILLED FISH

Serves: 6

INGREDIENTS

1 kg / 2.2 lb Fish (Sole), boneless, cut into square or rectangular pieces
2 tbsp / 30 ml / 1 fl oz Lemon (*nimbu*) juice
1 tsp / 3 gm Red chilli powder
1 tsp / 6 gm Ginger (*adrak*) paste
1 tsp / 6 gm Garlic (*lasan*) paste
1 tsp / 3 gm Cumin (*jeera*) powder
1 tbsp / 15 ml Olive oil
Salt to taste

METHOD

1 Mix all the ingredients together and marinate the fish for 1 hour.

2 Grill the fish in a microwave till golden brown. Turning once.

3 Serve hot.

Note: Chicken can be also cooked in the same way.

Chinar trees draped in snow in Srinagar.
Photograph: S. Irfan

142

Gaad Kaliya

FISH IN YELLOW GRAVY

Serves: 6

INGREDIENTS

1 kg / 2.2 lb Fish (*Sole / Rohu / Singada*), cut into slices
2 tsp / 6 gm Turmeric (*haldi*) powder
2 tbsp / 30 ml / 1 fl oz Mustard oil
Salt to taste
1 tsp / 2 gm Cumin (*jeera*) seeds
½ tsp Asafoetida (*hing*)
3 tsp / 9 gm Fennel (*saunf*) powder
2 tsp / 6 gm Ginger powder (*sonth*)
5 Green chillies

METHOD

1 Sprinkle 1 tsp turmeric powder all over the fish and keep aside for 1 hour.

2 Heat the oil in a pressure cooker; add salt, cumin seeds, asafoetida, 6 cups water, 1 tsp turmeric powder, fennel powder, and ginger powder. Bring to the boil, add fish and pressure cook for 5 minutes.

3 Open the lid and add green chillies. Cook again on high heat for 5 minutes. Serve with rice.

A potter at work in the 1920's.

One of the several bridges
on the River Jhelum.

All photographs courtesy Sarla Razdan

ISBN: 978-81-7436-692-4
© Sarla Razdan 2011

Published in India by
Roli Books Pvt Ltd
M-75, Greater Kailash-II Market,
New Delhi 110 048, India.
Phone: ++91-11-4068 2000
Fax: ++91-11-29217185
Email: info@rolibooks.com;
Website: www.rolibooks.com

Editor: Neeta Datta
Design: Supriya Saran, Divya Bhardwaj

Printed and bound in China